Encyclopedia of
Victorian Colored Pattern Glass
Book III

Syrups, Sugar Shakers & Cruets
From A to Z

by william heacock

Photography by
Richardson Printing Corporation
Marietta, Ohio

Published & Distributed by:

ANTIQUE PUBLICATIONS

W. R. Heacock

Box 655

Marietta, Ohio 45750

Price—$12.95
Limited Edition Hardbound—$16.95
price guide—$1.00

OTHER BOOKS BY WILLIAM HEACOCK

Encyclopedia of	Encyclopedia of
VICTORIAN COLORED PATTERN GLASS	VICTORIAN COLORED PATTERN GLASS
Book 1—Toothpick Holders	Book 2—Opalescent Glass
Softbound—$9.95	Softbound—$12.95

TO TED and RUTH

Whose kindness I'll never forget

TABLE OF CONTENTS

FOREWORD

This is the third volume in a series devoted to the identification and documentation of Victorian colored glass, primarily devoting attention to the years 1885 to 1910.

Book 3 is an in-depth study of colored glass syrup pitchers and sugar shakers with an addenda on cruets. These lovely pieces of glass were popular tableware during those long-lost years of elegant dining. They were usually a small part of a large matching service (thus the term "pattern glass"), which makes this book a valuable reference for pattern identification. You do not have to collect syrups, sugar shakers or cruets to enjoy this volume.

Book 4 is now in production and will cover patterns and novelties made in the extremely popular "custard" glass. Later volumes in this series will cover other specific fields.

HOW TO USE THIS BOOK

This book is divided into 5 basic sections. The first section of general text contains valuable information concerning my research and its results. Section 2 illustrates and identifies the syrups and sugar shakers together, since they are usually sought by today's collectors simultaneously. They could have been separated into two different chapters, but then there would have been too much duplication of data, since a great number of syrups are shown with their matching sugar shaker. The third section is an addenda on cruets, which includes only those cruets which are not included in the fine publication "More Cruets Only" by Dean L. Murray, or those about which updated information needed to be presented. Section 4 is a rather comprehensive re-print of several early ads and catalogues which illustrate and identify data of interest to collectors of early colored glass. Finally, I offer a listing of additions and corrections to the texts of Books I and II of this series, as well as an index to the first three volumes.

The pieces are illustrated primarily in alphabetical order, except for the late additions, milk glass and an occasional error in arrangement. Appropriate historical data is located at the bottom of each page. Each piece is given a figure number for easy reference when corresponding or advertising.

Since this series now numbers three volumes, and hopefully some day will number 10-12, reference numbers should be preceded by the number of the volume (example: Heacock 2-191 would refer the reader to Book 2, Figure 191, a green opalescent Wild Bouquet cruet). This provides a maximum of description with a minimum of words.

ACKNOWLEDGEMENTS

What started out as a minor entry into this series consisting of contributions from four major collectors mushroomed into a major publication in which two dozen people participated. Thanks to their unselfish loans of glass from their collections, this volume has become a treasure and a joy to produce.

Once again there are those, for reasons of their own, who wish to remain nameless in these acknowledgements. It is difficult to properly express my appreciation for their support when I cannot pinpoint their individual contribution to this book. But they know who they are—and as they read this I hope they realize that the words "thank you" look small in print, and its full meaning cannot be expressed in simple words. This "thank you" comes from the heart. I am proud to have had the privilege of knowing and working with each and every one of you.

Except for the above unnamed, the majority of the items shown in Book 3 were borrowed from the collections of Jack and Julie Mavis, Forrest and Ruth Lytle, and Tom and Fern Wintermyre. Their contribution to making this book possible is mountainous. Their personal sacrifices were testament to their devotion to this book. Due to the extreme distances between collections, their borrowed pieces were out of their homes up to three weeks. Not one of them showed any hesitancy whatsoever, or any concern over the safety of their pieces. I am happy to report that their trust in me was rewarded with the safe return of every piece borrowed.

It is impossible for me to pinpoint everyone's individual contribution to this volume. I am afraid that I gush a bit too much—so these persons listed here can consider themselves fortunate that I did not single them out for individual praise. But I thank all of them for their help, their patience, their kindness, and especially their complete trust in allowing me to include their rarest pieces in this book:

Chris & Rena Reynolds	Glen Schlotfeldt
Robert & Pat Costa	Rosalyn Bloxom
Jeanne Brocke	The Coffey Family
Everett & Addie Miller	Ruby Propst
Helen Wagner	Rudolph Evers
Ray & Jennie Goldsberry	Mrs. D. H. Flora
Marge Bartels	Mr. & Mrs. John Bowers
Emmett Craft	And most of all—Elnora Murray
Donald & Kathleen Carney	

A very, very special thank you must be extended to Jack Burk and Marilyn Johnson, both of whom ran tremendous risk in mailing their rare examples to me for inclusion in this book. Certainly one must realize that this took a little more time and effort than from those who had their pieces picked up personally. It also tremendously increased the chance of loss or breakage, so in a way I owe them a much bigger thank you. Alas, again it is impossible to find the special words to show my appreciation to these two fine people.

One individual deserves a special accommodation here. Tom Neale, a collector and dealer from Virginia, offered unlimited assistance when he learned about this project a mere two weeks before photography was scheduled to begin. He unselfishly travelled to the homes of several Virginia collectors, asking for their support by providing rare or unlisted examples—and personally vouching for their safe return himself. He gathered together more than 100 examples which he knew I needed and drove them up to the studio in Marietta himself in order to make the deadline. As I told Tom—what would have been a good book turned into a great book because of his help. I am proud to have him as a friend.

A special thank you to Fred Bickenheuser for his help in providing catalogues for my research. It was also through Fred that I learned about the location of some priceless old journals stashed in two library archives.

Again I find myself thanking the Oglebay Institute Mansion Museum and its curator John A. Artzberger for their permission to photograph and reprint catalogues which they have in their collection. This superior museum is only a few minutes off Interstate 70 at Oglebay Park in Wheeling, W. Va. It would be a stop you would never forget should you ever be traveling across this country's main artery.

This book was photographed in less than 3 days without the slightest loss of quality due to the tremendous abilities of the photographer, Dale Brown. My warmest thanks to him—and also to Dave Richardson and the top-drawer staff of Richardson Printing Corporation, who manage to take the garbled mess of this non-writer and turn it into something worthwhile.

My closing thank you is extended to two truly wonderful people who have been with me from the very beginning of this series, who offered unlimited encouragement when the obstacles seemed insurmountable, who shared every joy, as well as every failure, and who always held out a warm hand of welcome as I traveled back and forth from endless sessions with a printer 400 miles from home. I owe these two much more than I can ever hope to repay, and it is because of this that I am dedicating this book to my dearest friends, Ted and Ruth Heischman.

NOTES OF INTEREST FOR SYRUP COLLECTORS

Of the three items featured in this volume, the syrup pitchers have been popular tableware the longest. Some are available in the early flint and Sandwich patterns. They are quite rare in color, and not considered Victorian glass. However, there are examples in this book of patterns which were introduced as early as 1875, when colored tableware in massed produced quantities first started to appear.

According to some of the old catalogues reprinted in this volume, syrup pitchers (called "syrups" for short) were originally called molasses cans. Sometimes they are also called syrup jugs.

Syrups were not only made in glass. One collector has over 500—many in silver, silver-plate, pewter, pottery, china, majolica, and even Wedgewood.

Many syrups have sugar shakers available in the same pattern. However, this primarily only applies to the blown varieties. Very few pressed patterns were even made in sugar shakers. Sugar shakers were strictly Victorian in concept and use, and their life was limited as a mass produced item, whereas the syrup had a long productive life. A quick check of "items made" under the historical data will reveal whether a sugar shaker was made to match your syrup.

Production of colored glass syrups continued on past the Victorian era, yet on a considerably limited scale. This explains why so few syrups were made in the popular iridescent glass. The syrups of the depression era were designed in styles and colors that are foreign to earlier glass, with metal spring lids nothing like those shown within the pages of this book. Due to the rising popularity of colored glass, a few reproductions have appeared in the past decade to haunt collectors, but most are exposed within the pages of this book.

SYRUP TOPS—ORIGINAL, REPLACED OR REPRODUCTION???

Most colored glass syrups had metal tops applied to them with plaster. These tops were made out of tin, pewter and other types of nickel or silver-plated metal. Frequently syrups are found by collectors today with a badly decomposed top—or even no top at all. This has created a need for metal tops to replace the missing top. These tops are now being reproduced, in at least two known versions. One is poor in quality, is very shiny and quite obviously a reproduction (Fig. 249 top). The other is pewter-like, good quality, has an old look—but unfortunately is not old (Fig. 123 top).

Deciding whether a syrup has an original top or not is determined by two major methods. The first is to study the inner rim and check for darkened plaster. The best method is to compare the lid to an old ad or catalogue reprint. However, neither of these methods is entirely fool-proof, as there are *always* exceptions. And to this author, as long as the syrup has a decent top on it, whether original, replaced or a reproduction, the value of the piece of glass which it caps should not be affected.

This book should not be used to determine if the top on your syrup is original. Many of the pieces shown here have their original spring tops, but several do not. I toyed with the idea of noting "original" or "not original" tops, but soon realized that I would be adding fuel to the fire concerning the impression some collectors have concerning its importance. The next time you see a rare syrup with a reproduction top on it, and you feel a few qualms about buying it, just ask yourself how a piece of glass could last so long undamaged—whereas the much stronger and more resistant (to breakage) metal top didn't make it.

THE SUGAR SHAKER SYNDROME

The dispenser which is commonly called a sugar shaker today was originally called a sugar sifter or sugar duster. They are also often referred to today as muffineers, but this label is usually reserved for the foreign varieties. These highly collectible charmers first appeared to any degree in the mid 1880's, primarily in blown glass. Following their popular introduction, several pressed glass sugar shakers began to appear, but only for a short while. Sugar shakers can also be found in china, silver-plate, silver, cut glass, and even majolica.

Many syrup collectors have turned to sugar shakers as a sideline collection, often trying to match them up to patterns in syrups. Their connection escapes me, except perhaps that they were both used to sweeten food. No matter, they have both found their way into the hearts of hundreds of collectors, and deservingly so.

The life of the pattern glass sugar shaker was very short, lasting almost as long as the pattern glass toothpick—from circa 1885 to 1905. There are the usual exceptions, of course. After 1905, the china sugar shaker emerged as a substitute for the glass type.

The tops were either good quality pewter or a lesser quality tin, which is often found today rusty with corroded threads. However, sugar shakers were a passing fancy and often impractical for table usage, so most were put away on a shelf for safe keeping. Perhaps that is why so few sugar shakers are found today with the usual usage and age wear, whereas the syrups are often found cloudy, scratched, and sometimes faded (on color-flashed glass).

Due to the rising popularity of sugar shakers, reproductions are plaguing the market. The tops are also being reproduced in a very convincing "aged" metal. An old top adds a little special appeal to an old sugar shaker, but it should not be considered any less valuable because the shaker has a reproduction top on it. The old tops sell for $5 to $10, but are very hard to find any more, so never pass up a good rare old sugar shaker just because the top is replaced. You can always switch tops with a lesser pattern.

A TOUGH JOB MADE EASIER—FURTHER ACKNOWLEDGEMENTS

This certainly has been a productive year for this author. In 14 months I produced three books, more than 40 columns, and kept my small antique business in the black as well. And yet none of this would have been possible were it not for the help I have received in my research efforts. True, I have spent endless hours going through the archives of university libraries, studying private collections, corresponding with other authors (a few of whom refused to offer any assistance to me at all), and traveling to glass museums. But the majority of my major discoveries resulted from unbelievably kind offers of assistance and trust.

Certainly one of my major research coups was when I began corresponding with D. L. Helman of Indiana, Pa. He had confirmed an attribution made in one of my columns, informing me that he had found shards of the Nestor pattern at North wood's old Indiana (Pa.) plant site—where a football field rests today. He very kindly offered to send these few shards to me for inspection and analysis. As wonderful and important as these few shards were, luck was with us, and a flower bed was being dug up at the site. Through the additional efforts of Mr. Helman's father, Harry A. Helman, and good friend, George McMillan, several additional boxes full of glass were turned up, washed and sent to me for inspection. These hunks of glass, of absolutely no pecuniary value, were like a gold mine to me—and I was quite thrilled when Mr. Helman told me to just keep the shards, since they would mean much more to me than to him. I will remain forever in his debt, and his contribution to glass documentation will be remembered by thousands.

Equally as exciting was having two huge U. S. Glass Company catalogues loaned to me for photostating. They are now a permanent record on film, and I will be sharing many of these priceless pages with you in a later volume of this series (many of the syrups in the reprints here were lifted from this catalogue). This privilege was given so generously by Fred Bickenheuser. Another exciting "find" was an old catalogue (circa 1885) of the Belmont Glass Company of Bellaire, Ohio. Several patterns (i.e. Pilgrim Bottle) are attributed here for the first time ever, thanks to the chance I was given to study this catalogue. A possible reprint is under negotiation, but there are extraneous circumstances which make it impossible right now. However, the documentation is the most important factor right now, and I truly appreciate the most gracious opportunity I was given to even just see the catalogue.

I have repeatedly thanked the Oglebay Institute for their most generous help in allowing study and reprints of the catalogues which they have from the old Hobbs, Jefferson & Beaumont Glass Companies. They also have granted permission to include items from their extensive glass collection in this series, and I look forward with great anticipation to this opportunity.

A final chunk of my research findings resulted from the dozens of letters I receive every week from readers who seem to know how deep my desire is to know all the facts—no matter how minor they may seem to them. Due to this unbelievable growth of volume in mail, it is now virtually impossible for me to personally answer every letter received. Those which can be answered are often two to three weeks delayed. So to all of you who have written, please accept my sincerest of thanks, and to those who received no reply, please accept my sincerest apologies.

REPRODUCTIONS—A Note of Encouragement

As I write this, things are looking a little brighter for glass collectors who live in constant peril of reproductions. We are small in number, and getting legislation to protect our investments has been a long, frustrating battle. Congress seems to be more concerned with "the masses" and their needs (or votes), so our little, seemingly unimportant, glass reproduction Bill is constantly shuffled to the bottom of the priority stack.

Yet in 1975 we made several encouraging steps. We now have a "lobby" for our cause, an organization of devoted glass collectors called "G.L.A.S.S." (Glass Legislative Action Security Society). This fine group of people are our voice in Washington, and rather than a pilfering of letters and petitions dripping into non-influential offices, all material can be sent directly to G.L.A.S.S. and be routed to the bureaucratic committee of most importance at a time where our cries will be heard to better advantage. I donate all my speaking fees to this worthwhile group, and urge all organizations of collectors to do the same with portions of their treasury. Money is needed to defray small operating expenses, since everyone involved in this fight is a volunteer. Send your letters, your petitions, and donations to G.L.A.S.S., 6213 Joyce Drive, Washington, D.C. 20031.

Also in 1975, the glass reproduction bill was assigned a new number, H.R. 6500. This is nothing unusual—the same bill has had several numbers assigned to it in past years. But, in yet another encouraging step, this bill now has a co-sponsor (besides the patient Congressman Fred Rooney), Congresswoman Marjorie Holt. Perhaps the Bicentennial will bring on a wave of desire to preserve our posterity, and it will become illegal to reproduce anything of antique value without permanently dating the imitation.

A very minor sign of encouragement came in 1975 when I was contacted by the ABC News "Close-up" staff, which wanted to interview me concerning the problem of reproductions among dealers and collectors. They flew a crew in from Chicago and interviewed me for three hours. I stressed the importance of passage of this most important bill, but they seemed more impressed by the difference in value between two items which looked exactly alike in their untrained eyes. Thus, the final edited report was nothing more than a small wave in an ocean of protest. They completely misinterpreted the purpose of the interview. The broadcast didn't even reach half of the country, since many large cities opted for local programming. Needless to say, our fight for passage of this legislation is only beginning. Even a news team as expert as ABC's thought the crisis of minor importance, cutting this long interview down to 2-1/2 minutes of edited film.

Finally, a great deal of praise must be extended to the editorial staff of the Antique Trader Weekly, which has taken a strong stand in support of Bill H.R. 6500, even though a considerable amount of their advertising dollar comes from distributors of this new glass. They sent out thousands of petitions to dealers, many of which were returned with signatures, gathered together and forwarded to appropriate channels in Washington. They cannot be commended enough for their courageous stand.

Hopefully, as you read this years from now, you can look on it as a dated piece of triviality from this author. It will seem minor and "soap-boxish" after this bill is passed into law, but if this editorial causes just one reader to write their Congressman (or G.L.A.S.S.), then it would be worth the cost of the extra page it took to include it in this volume.

THE NORTHWOOD-DUGAN DIGGINGS

The 1975 diggings at the Indiana, Pa. factory site of the Northwood Company are responsible for a considerable updating of information on a few patterns which I had incorrectly attributed to other companies. However, it was equally responsible for confirmation of many of my "theoretical" attributions—such as S-Repeat, Nestor and Fan.

The variety of patterns and colors to be found among these shards is almost staggering. I am sifting through them now as I write this. However, it is impossible to definitely attribute any of these patterns singly to Northwood, for he only operated this factory from 1895 to 1901 (his last two years as a member factory of the National Glass Company). After Northwood pulled out, the factory retained his name. In fact, in 1902 there were *two* plants carrying the Northwood title. With the onset of financial troubles for the big National Glass combine, in January 1904 the plant was leased out to its managers, Thomas E. Dugan and W. G. Minnemeyer, and the name of the company immediately changed. The new firm continued production of many of the original Northwood molds, in colors which were distinctive of the Northwood "touch." This was no doubt due to the retention of trained personnel familiar with the procedures used in the production of quality colored tableware. Around 1913 the name of the company was changed to the Diamond Glassware Company, and a trademark—the D-within-a-Diamond—was registered. The company burned to the ground in June, 1931, and was never rebuilt.

Thus, I have hundreds of shards in patterns and colors which I am not familiar with, as they are of much later vintage. Also, it is difficult to determine exactly which pattern was made by Northwood, which by Dugan, which by Diamond and which by a combination of two or more.

I am preparing a massive publication on Northwood's glass and I will later delve deeper into these confusions and offer a documentative analysis, but for now, I feel my readers are entitled to know which patterns and colors were found at this factory site.

The following is a comprehensive listing of these shards:

DAISY & FERN—several pieces in this, in blue, crnbry, white

DIAMOND SPEARHEAD—2 pcs. here, quite large, in vaseline opal.

FLUTED SCROLLS—many pcs., in blue, crystal, vas.

JACKSON—part of a butter lid, salt shaker, in custard

CIRCLED SCROLL—a big pc. from a sauce, in green

LOUIS XV—so many pcs., all in custard

COINSPOT—many pcs. in crnbry, blue, white opales.

JEWELLED HEART—a huge chunk from a crystal water pitcher; a rare piece in custard

WILD BOUQUET—three pcs., one in white opales., 2 in custard

PANELLED SPRIG—pcs. in cranberry & with opal. criss-cross

SPANISH LACE—a dozen pieces in blue, crnbry, white, and canary

CHRYSANTHEMUM SPRIG—big chunk in custard, several in blue custard

INVERTED FAN & FEATHER—2 good pieces in pink slag, a blue finial, a big piece from custard butter lid

FAN—a great big piece from the water pitcher base

TOWN PUMP—a complete handle from this in blue

OPALESCENT STRIPE—several in white, blue, crnbry

OPALESCENT SWIRL—several in crnbry, blue

S REPEAT—stopper in green, salt shaker bottom in blue

ARGONAUT SHELL—base to a spooner in crystal (probably opal top)

KEYHOLE—a piece in blue

CABBAGE LEAF—two legs, one in blue—another in green (could also be *Winter Cabbage*)

DOLPHIN COMPOTE—a big chunk from the dolphin's body in blue

BLOCKED THUMBPRINT & BEADS—a piece in clear

WREATHED CHERRY—a large piece in amethyst carnival, another in crystal

REFLECTING DIAMONDS—nice piece in green

Although carnival glass is not my research field, listed here are a few patterns which I was able to identify.

HEAVY IRIS (Har Car 4, 51)—in marigold

VINEYARD (Har Car 2, 118)—in marigold

WOVEN TWIGS (Pres. 2, 77)—amethyst

BASKETWEAVE (Pres. 1, #12)—white carnival

APPLE BLOSSOMS (Pres. 1, #5)—a piece in amethyst & marigold

WINDFLOWER—in white carnival (see Book 2)

Many of the patterns listed above have been credited only to Northwood by myself and others. These shards, and the confusion and questions they now bring collectors of Northwood glass, will be dealt with further in a later volume of this series.

THE FRUSTRATIONS IN PROVIDING DOCUMENTED RESEARCH DATA

The one thing I have learned this year which overshadows everything else I learned is that it is almost impossible to assume that a certain company made a certain pattern because the colors, patterns or shapes are similar. This is a very valuable form of providing additional documentation, but it should not be used as the sole source.

The recent Indiana, Pa. diggings were a shattering blow to my previously reported findings—despite the fact that they also added valuable documentation to several of my theories. I don't mind admitting a mistake, but it is possible that this writer and a few other glass historians are going to have to add more than just a few corrections to previously printed documentation.

Dozens and dozens of shards in carnival glass were found at this Pennsylvania plant site. It is generally agreed that carnival (iridescent) glass first made its popular appearance around 1905. A few companies have been properly credited with carnival production: Northwood (Wheeling), Fenton, Imperial, Cambridge, and Millersburg Glass Companies. But the too-long overlooked Dugan Glass Company (1904-1912) and (later called the) Diamond Glass-Ware Company are going to have to be added now to that impressive list of quality glassmakers of the early twentieth century.

An example of further confusion is the *Corn Vase* (opalescent version) which both Hartung and Presnick attributed to Northwood, and this is probably very likely true—if the mold was made before 1901. However, the 1905 Butler Brothers ad in Book 2, pg. 74, which I attributed to Northwood because of the *Corn Vase*, was more likely a display of glass from the Dugan Glass Company. I have shards from the 1975 diggings in both *Keyhole & Reflecting Diamonds*. With no bona fide proof that the *Corn Vase* is actually Northwood (Presnick reports a signed piece, but this could probably pre-date Northwood's 1901 departure from this company), then I feel that Dugan should be credited with most of the production of this pattern. The carnival version of the *Corn Vase* (with the Northwood trademark) is not even similar.

Thus, you can see how easy it is to fall for previous research reports. Just because it is in print doesn't make it fact. Remember this—even as you read this series.

THE VALUE AND RARITY GUIDES—An Explanation

The little guide which I print to accompany each volume in this series has come under considerable discussion and criticism of late, and I felt a few words concerning their importance, their purpose and their meaning were necessary. Some say they are not necessary, others say they hurt the market, and many others use them unwisely. Still others claim the prices are too high, others too low, and I have received complaints because I do not provide prices for colors other than those illustrated as figures in the book.

In answer to this criticism, I ask that you look at the title of the little booklet. It is called a "value" guide—not a "price" guide. I have long criticized the use of price guides other than just that—a guide. All you have to do is ask any professional antique dealer about the leading price guides and they all have very strong opinions about them. I find them almost useless as the editors usually raise their prices about 10% every two years, whereas the glass in my field has increased over 35% in that same period. It is frustrating when trying to sell an item to a collector who carries his guide around with him. Fortunately, this market today is made up of an elite, large group of educated individuals who have studied prices at shows and in the finer shops, and have become aware of market values. I am, of course, referring to collectors of colored Victorian pattern glass—but I am certain that these conditions are similar in the art glass, Sandwich glass, and even depression glass fields.

But the big difference here is that prices in those fields are well advertised, well-known and watched closely by editors of major price guides. This is where my guides have a specialized field virtually to themselves. They can offer figures on collectible items not listed (according to true market trends) anywhere else.

I called the listing a "value" guide to try and dispel the common practice of lifting figures right out of the book when pricing an item for sale. For dealers and collectors who do that, the chances are strong that they are pricing a "shelf-sitter." As a collector and dealer and student of market trends, I can offer you an estimate of "full retail value," but I cannot guarantee you a sale at that price. The secret to an item's salability is *how* many people with *how* much money want that item *how* badly. Add to this *how* rare it is, and you come up with an idea of what the item will sell for. If my book was a "price" guide, then maybe I would have quoted you prices for retail sales. But what I was quoting was full retail, and most dealers know that few collectors wish to pay an item's full value—*we all* would like some kind of bargain. Collectors prefer something more for their money than having to pay book price. So please don't turn on this author if you can't get that much for your item, or if you paid more than that for yours, or if you have become a victim of a dealer using my price guide.

So what is the purpose of my guide? It offers you two services at least—if not more. It offers you a ceiling on what you can pay without being "stung." Also it offers you some proof of value in case of loss for insurance claims. In some cases where the rarity guide comes in, determining value is difficult. In all honesty, many rare items are priceless and worth whatever a collector is willing to pay. But no matter how beautiful an item is, no matter how perfect, no matter what color—if no one wants it for that price, then it is not worth it, no matter what anyone's price guide says.

Forgive the editorial sound of this essay. I wish I could discontinue the controversy by eliminating the price guides altogether, but that would shave a considerable portion of the limited market my books already have.

GLASS COMPANIES WHICH MANUFACTURED TWO OR MORE ITEMS SHOWN IN THIS BOOK

Below is a listing of the glass companies which are represented in this book, and the location of their plant. I am listing them here in order to save their lengthy, wordy inclusion all over the book.

Beaumont Glass Company, Martins Ferry, Ohio
Dithridge & Co. (operated the Fort Pitt Glass Works), Pittsburgh, Pa.
Fostoria Glass Co., Moundsville, W. Va.
Gillinder & Sons, Philadelphia, Pa.
Consolidated Lamp & Glass Co., at Fostoria, O. & Coraopolis, Pa.
U.S. Glass Company (20 different factories) Home office: Pittsburgh, Pa.
A. H. Heisey Glass Co., Newark, Ohio
A. J. Beatty Glass Co., Steubenville & Tiffin, Ohio
George Duncan Sons & Co. (later Duncan & Miller)
Riverside Glass Works, Wellsburg, W. Va.
Columbia Glass Co., Findlay, Ohio
Hobbs, Brockunier & Co. (later Hobbs Glass Co.), Wheeling, W. Va.
Indiana Tumbler & Goblet Co., Greentown, Pa.
Challinor, Taylor & Co., Pittsburgh, Pa.
Buckeye Glass Co., Martins Ferry, Ohio
McKee & Brothers, Pittsburgh & later Jeanette, Pa.
West Virginia Glass Co., Martins Ferry, Ohio
Pittsburgh Lamp, Brass & Glass Co., Pittsburgh, Pa. (Dithridge joined this with Kopp)
Tarentum Glass Co., Tarentum, Pa.
Belmont Glass Co., Bellaire, Ohio
Bellaire Goblet Co., Findlay, Ohio

ABBREVIATION KEYS

opales. — opalescent
crnbry — cranberry
vas. — vaseline
Y.O.P. — Year (or Years) of Production
t.p. — toothpick holder
salt — salt shaker (not salt dip)
repro — reproduction
mini — miniature
illus. — illustrated or illustration
decor. — decorated or decoration
jelly — jelly compote
prod. — produced or production
Orig. — original
Mfr. — manufacturer
ref. — refer or reference
IVT — Inverted Thumbprint
Fig. — Figure
pg. — page
o.s. — original stopper
n.o.s. — not original stopper

BIBLIOGRAPHY REFERENCES

BAR	—Barrett, Richard C.	"Popular American Ruby-Stained Pattern Glass"	Forward's Color Productions, Inc., Manchester, Vt.
BOND	—Bond, Marcelle	"The Beauty of Albany Glass"	Publishers Printing House, Berne, Ind.
HAR CAR	Hartung, Marion	Series of 10 Books on Carnival Glass	Author
HEACOCK I	—Heacock, William	"Encyclopedia of Victorian Colored Pattern Glass" Volume I	Author
HEACOCK II	—Heacock, William	"Encyclopedia of Victorian Colored Pattern Glass" Volume II	Author
HER	—Herrick, Dr. Ruth	"Greentown Glass"	
HAR OP	—Hartung, Marion T.	"Opalescent Pattern Glass"	Wallace-Homestead Co., Des Moines, Iowa
HAR NOR	Hartung, Marion T.	"Northwood Pattern Glass in Color"	
KAMM	—Kamm, Minnie W.	Series of 8 books on Pattern Glass	Kamm Publications, Grosse Pt., Mich.
LEE EAPG	—Lee, Ruth Webb	"Early American Pressed Glass"	Lee Publications, Wellesley Hills, Mass.
LEE VG	—Lee, Ruth Webb	"Victorian Glass"	
METZ 1	Metz, Alice H.	"Early American Pattern Glass"	Author
METZ 2	Metz, Alice H.	"Much More Early American Pattern Glass"	
MILLER	—Miller, Everett & Addie	"The New Martinsville Glass Story"	Richardson Printing Marietta, O.
MUR CR	—Murray, Dean L.	"More Cruets Only"	Killgore Graphics, Inc., Phoenix, Ariz.
MUR FOS	Murray, Melvin	"History of Fostoria, Ohio Glass"	Gray Printing Co., Fostoria, Ohio
PET SAL	—Peterson, Arthur	"Glass Salt Shakers 1,000 Patterns"	Wallace-Homestead Co., Des Moines, Iowa
PET PAT	—Peterson, Arthur	"Glass Patents and Patterns"	Celery City Printing, Sanford, Fla.
PRES	—Presnick, Rose	"Carnival & Iridescent Glass"	Banner Printing, Wadsworth, Ohio
SM FIN	Smith, Don E.	"Findlay Pattern Glass"	Gray Printing Co., Fostoria, Ohio
SM MIN	—Smith, Frank R. & Ruth E.	"Miniature Lamps"	Thomas Nelson & Sons, Inc., New York, N.Y.
TAY	—Taylor, Ardelle	"Colored Glass Sugar Shakers & Syrup Pitchers"	Author
UNITT	—Unitt, Doris & Peter	"American & Canadian Goblets" "American & Canadian Goblets," Volume II	Clock House Petersborough, Ont., Can.

Syrups & Sugar Shakers in Color

Photo by Jack Hall Photography

RARE EMERALD GREEN
"PINEAPPLE & FAN"
(syrup)
A. H. HEISEY GLASS
CIRCA 1900

1	2	3	4	5
ACORN (blue)	**ACORN** (blue)	**ACORN** (emerald green)	**ACORN** (cranberry)	**ACORN** (black amethyst)

6	7	8	9	10
ALBA (custard)	**ALBA** (pink opaque)	**ALBA BLOSSOMS** (decorated milk)	**APPLE BLOSSOM** (decorated milk)	**APPLE BLOSSOM** (decorated milk)

ACORN (Figures 1-5)
Maker: Known prod. by Beaumont Glass Co., Martin's Ferry, O., with possible earlier production at Hobbs   **Y.O.P.:** from 1890 to 1900   **Colors made:** opaque colors of white, blue, black amethyst and a peach-blow-colored (not actually) pink blending to white—also crystal glass colors of blue, amethyst, apple green, clear and very rare in cranberry   **Items made:** syrup, sugar shaker, salt shaker, t.p.   **Repro's:** none   **Name by:** *Pet Sal*, pg. 21-A   **Note:** The toothpick & salt have never been reported in the crystal colors.

ALBA (Figures 6-7) (See also Fig. 348)
Maker: Dithridge   **Y.O.P.:** from 1894   **Colors made:** opaque white, blue, pink and custard yellow   **Items made:** syrup, salts, sugar shaker, and scarce in a table set   **Unreported:** toothpick   **Repro's:** none   **Name by:** *Kamm 8*, pg. 76.

ALBA BLOSSOMS (Figure 8)
Maker: Dithridge   **Y.O.P.:** circa 1895   **Colors made:** only decorated white opaque reported to date   **Items made:** syrup, sugar shaker   **Repro's:** none   **Name by:** *Author*.

APPLE BLOSSOM (Figures 9-10)
Maker: Northwood Co., Indiana, Pa.   **Y.O.P.:** circa 1896—see ad reprint Book 1, pg. 57   **Colors made:** decorated milk glass—the mold was also used in a *Daisy & Fern* variant (Fig. 88)   **Items made:** table set, water set, berry set, syrup, sugar shaker, salt, cruet, miniature lamp   **Unreported:** toothpick   **Repro's:** none   **Name by:** Original mfr. name   **Note:** Often confused for the popular *Cosmos* pattern.

11
ARGUS SWIRL
(cranberry)

12
ARGUS SWIRL
(cranberry)

13
ARGUS SWIRL
(peach bloom)

14
ARGUS SWIRL
(peach bloom)

15
ASTER & LEAF
(blue)

16
ASTER & LEAF
(emerald green)

17
AZTEC MEDALLION (SWIRL)
(green opal.)

18
BANDED BARREL
(amber)

19
BANDED PORTLAND
(rose-flashed)

20
BASKETWEAVE
(amber)

ARGUS SWIRL (Figures 11-14)
Maker: Probably Consolidated **Y.O.P.:** from 1894 to 1898 **Colors made:** opaque white, blue and pink blending to white—scarce in cranberry—experimental colors likely **Items made:** syrup, sugar shaker, salt, cruet, mustard **Repro's:** none **Name by:** *Warman* **Note:** the pink to white is sometimes confused for peachblow. Satin finish items scarce, and often priced as if they were New England peachblow.

ASTER & LEAF (Figures 15-16)
Maker: Beaumont's #217 **Y.O.P.:** circa 1895 **Other name:** *Tapered Vine* (Taylor) **Colors made:** emerald green, blue & cranberry **Items made:** syrup, sugar shaker, salts **Repro's:** none **Name by:** *Pet Sal*, pg. 21-J.

AZTEC MEDALLION (SWIRL) (Figure 17)
Maker: Unknown **Y.O.P.:** circa 1905 **Colors made:** illus. item only color reported, although white opales. likely **Items made:** only syrup seen **Repro's:** none **Name by:** *Author*.

BANDED BARREL (Figure 18)
Maker: Unknown **Y.O.P.:** circa 1895 **Colors:** amber, green, crystal **Items:** syrup illus. only item reported to date **Repro's:** none **Name by:** *Author*.

BANDED PORTLAND (Figure 19)
Maker: U.S. Glass #15071 pattern **Y.O.P.:** circa 1901 (see ad reprint, Book 1) **Other name:** *Virginia* (original "state" series name), also *Maiden's Blush* (Lee) **Colors made:** crystal and rose-flashed **Items made:** every shape imaginable, including punch bowl and cups **Repro's:** none **Name by:** *Metz 1*, pg. 197 **IMPORTANT NOTE:** This pattern has been attributed by some sources to the Portland Glass Co., circa 1870, yet is based on questionable evidence. If it *was* made there originally, and the molds later re-issued by U.S. Glass, it would not have been in the color-stained version. This pink-staining was characteristic of post-1900 patterns.

BASKETWEAVE (Figure 20)
Maker: Unknown, although Kamm hints it may be Sandwich, a poorly accepted theory **Y.O.P.:** circa 1885 **Colors made:** crystal, amber, blue, canary & apple green—also opaque white **Items made:** complete table service, except toothpick, cruet & other typical Victoriana **Repro's:** water pitcher, goblet & tray in certain colors **Name by:** *LEE EAPG*, plt. 104. **IMPORTANT NOTE:** Warman's 12th Edition lists the items in which this pattern was made on pg. 87—however, they unfortunately list them under the wrong pattern, a line Kamm calls *Open Basketweave*. This completely different pattern was not made in color at all.

21 BEADED SWAG (ruby-stain)
22 BEATTY RIB (blue opal.)
23 BEATTY HONEYCOMB (white opal.)
24 BEATTY SWIRL (blue opal.)
25 BLOCK BAND (marigold-flashed)
26 BLOCKED THUMBPRINT BAND (ruby-stain)

27 BLOWN TWIST (blue opal.)
28 BLOWN TWIST (blue opal.)
29 BRILLIANT (amber-stain)
30 BROKEN COLUMN (with red dots)
31 BROKEN COLUMN (with red dots)

BEADED SWAG (Figure 21)
Maker: Heisey   **Y.O.P.:** from 1897 to circa 1905   **Colors made:** crystal, ruby-stained, milk glass (Opal), emerald green, limited prod. in custard & vaseline   **Items:** almost every conceivable shape including wines, mugs, cups & saucers and 2 sizes of rose bowls   **Repro's:** none yet   **Name by:** Popular variation of Kamm's *Bead Swag*, Vol 2, pg. 75   **Note:** The syrup jug would be extremely rare in the last three colors listed.

BEATTY RIB (Figure 22)
Maker: Beatty   **Y.O.P.:** circa 1888   **Colors:** opalesc. white, blue and experimental canary   **Items made:** see listing in Book 2   **Repro's:** an ash tray   **Name by:** *LEE EAPG*, plt. 69   **Note:** Book 2, Fig. 213 is the covered butter. I had been told incorrectly that it was the covered powder jar. Reference *Lee*.

BEATTY HONEYCOMB (Figure 23)
Maker: Beatty   **Y.O.P.:** circa 1888 to 1895   **Colors:** white and blue opalescent   **Items made:** see listing Book 2—the illustrated rare sugar shaker above was inadvertently omitted from that list   **Repro's:** rose bowl, pulled vase, baskets in blue & green opales.   **Name by:** *LEE VG*, pg. 218.

BEATTY SWIRL (Figure 24)
Maker: Beatty   **Y.O.P.:** circa 1889   **Colors made:** white, blue and rare in canary opalescent   **Items made:** see list book 2   **Repro's:** None   **Name by:** a popular shortened version of Kamm's *Beatty Swirled Opal*, her Vol. 8   **Note:** the syrup illus. above is very rare.

BLOCK BAND (Figure 25)
Maker: Geo. Duncan Sons & Co., #27 pattern   **Y.O.P.:** circa 1890 to 1900's   **Colors made:** crystal, ruby-stained and marigold-flashed (illus.)   **Items made:** considerable variety — no toothpick seen to date   **Repro's:** none   **Name by:** *Kamm 3*, pg. 132   **Note:** a souvenir wine, dated 1914, is shown in Barret. Often early patterns were re-issued later as souvenir ware. Take care when referring to this pattern — Kamm inadvertently gave a different pattern the same name in her Book 7, pg. 20.

BLOCKED THUMBPRINT BAND (Figure 26)
Maker: Still speculative—likely U.S. Glass   **Y.O.P.:** circa 1900   **Colors made:** crystal & ruby-stained   **Items made:** t.p., ind. creamer & sugar, syrup, cruet — usually as souvenirs   **Repro's:** none to date known   **Name by:** *Author*—Book 1

BLOWN TWIST (Figures 27-28)
Maker: Primarily Northwood at several of his locations   **Y.O.P.:** circa 1892 to 1905   **Colors made:** white, blue, canary & green opalescent—cranberry would be scarce   **Items made:** sugar shaker, water set—no syrup has been documented to date, as incorrectly listed in Book 2—add a celery vase to that listing   **Repro's:** a similar pattern was made by Fenton in several novelty items—see Book 2   **Name by:** *Har Op*, pg. 19.

(continued next page)

32
BUBBLE LATTICE
(cranb. glossy)

33
BUBBLE LATTICE
(rubina)

34
BUBBLE LATTICE
(cranb. satin)

35
BULBOUS BASE OPTIC
(cranberry)

36
BULBOUS BASE
(northwood mosaic)

37
BULGING LOOPS
(yellow cased)

38
BULGING LOOPS
(pink cased)

39
BULGING LOOPS
(pidgeon blood)

40
BULGING MIDRIFF
(amber)

41
BULLSEYE & BUTTONS
(emerald)

(continued from previous page)

BRILLIANT (Figure 29)
Maker: Riverside **Y.O.P.:** circa 1897 **Colors:** crystal, ruby & amber-stained **Items:** table, water & berry set, t.p., syrup, goblet, wine, celery, salt, indiv. creamer & open sugar, possibly others **Other name:** *Petalled Medallion* **Repro's:** none **Name by:** Orig. Mfr. name.

BROKEN COLUMN (Figures 30-31)
Maker: Columbia Glass, with continued production by U.S. Glass **Y.O.P.:** from 1887 to circa 1900 **Other names:** *Notched Rib, Rattan* and *Bamboo* **Colors:** crystal, ruby-stained & very rare in cobalt blue **Items:** too numerous to mention — toothpick not yet documented **Repro's:** new goblets by L. G. Wright (crystal only) **Name by:** *Millard* **Notes:** This pattern has also been attributed to Portland Glass Co., a theory which only the most devoted Portland collectors accept. At any rate, this early company could not possibly have made the colored pieces.

BUBBLE LATTICE (Figures 32-34)
Maker: All evidence points to Hobbs **Y.O.P.:** circa 1890 (see Book 2) **Colors made:** white, blue, cranberry, canary & rubina opales., sometimes satin finished **Items made:** table set, water set, berry set, cruet, t.p., syrup, sugar shakers (2 shapes), salts, finger bowl **Repro's:** oddities by Fenton — not in original shapes however **Name by:** *Author* **Other names:** "Bubble" *(Pet Sal)*, "Plaid" *(Har Op)*.

BULBOUS BASE (Figures 35-36)
Maker: originally by Hobbs, #311 Ware **Y.O.P.:** circa 1890 **Colors**

made: cranberry & crystal—very rare in purple slag **Items made:** complete table service in the first two colors **Repro's:** none **Name by:** *Author* **Note:** The syrup illustration here has an unusual optic effect in the glass. The mold for this pattern was also used on the *Seaweed & Coinspot* patterns (Figures 54 & 279). The purple slag was probably a Northwood re-issue. See catalogue reprint on page 65.

BULGING LOOPS (Figures 37-39)
Maker: Consolidated Lamp & Glass **Y.O.P.:** from 1894 to 1905 **Colors made:** cased & opaque white, blue, green, yellow & pink — cranberry & pigeon blood — experimental colors & sometimes satin finished **Items made:** table, water & berry set, cruet, t.p., syrup, mustard, salts, sugarshaker **Repro's:** none **Name by:** *Boultinghouse.*

BULGING MIDRIFF (Figure 40)
Maker: Belmont Glass Co. #96 Pattern **Y.O.P.:** circa 1885 **Colors made:** vaseline & amber known — possibly blue & apple green as well **Items known:** syrup & sugar shaker **Other name:** Taylor calls this *Two Band Inverted Thumbprint* **Repro's:** none **Name by:** *Author.*

BULLSEYE & BUTTONS (Figure 41)
Maker: Only speculative at this point **Y.O.P.:** circa 1895 **Colors made:** crystal & emerald green **Items known:** a syrup, cruet, t.p. only items documented to date **Repro's:** None **Name by:** *Murray,* Book 2 **Note:** Very similar to *Dew & Raindrop,* but the patterns are not the same at all.

42
BUTTON ARCHES
(ruby-stain)

43
CACTUS
(chocolate)

44
CARMEN
(amber-stain)

45
CHALLINOR'S #313
(blue opaque)

46
**CHALLINOR'S
FORGET-ME-NOT**
(pink)

47
**CHALLINOR'S
FORGET-ME-NOT**
(butterscotch)

48
CHAMPION
(amber-stain)

49
**CHRYSANTHEMUM-
BASE SWIRL**
(blue glossy)

50
**CHRYSANTHEMUM-
BASE SWIRL**
(turquoise satin)

51
**CHRYSANTHEMUM-
BASE SPECKLED**
(cranberry)

52
**CHRYSANTHEMUM-
BASE SPECKLED**
(blue)

BUTTON ARCHES (Figure 42)
Maker: Originally by Duncan, then by U.S. Glass (which absorbed Duncan) and later again by Duncan after he established a new company at Washington, Pa. **Y.O.P.:** From 1885 to as late as 1915 — continued production as souvenir ware **Colors made:** crystal, ruby-stained and souvenirs in clambroth opaque **Items made:** complete table service **Repro's:** new t.p., covered butter and wines on the market now — also indiv. creamer and goblet **Name by:** *Kamm 1*, pg. 111.

CACTUS (Figure 43)
Maker: Indiana Tumbler & Goblet **Y.O.P.:** 1900 to 1903 **Colors made:** crystal and chocolate glass — experimental production in other colors **Items made:** complete service including cracker jar **Repro's:** new toothpicks in all colors imaginable by St. Clair — the vaseline opalescent items found were all made by Fenton in the early sixties **Other name:** *Panelled Agave* (Kamm) **Name by:** *Herr.*, pg. 24 **Note:** The syrup has never been reproduced.

CARMEN (Figure 44)
Maker: Fostoria Glass Co., Moundsville **Y.O.P.:** circa 1897 **Other names:** *Fostoria #575, Panelled Diamonds & Finecut* **Colors made:** crystal and decorated with amber-stained flower sprays **Items made:** complete table set **Repro's:** none **Name by:** Orig. Mfr. name (*Kamm 5*, pg. 121).

CHALLINOR'S #313 (Figure 45)
Maker: Challinor, Taylor & Co. (continued by U.S. Glass) **Y.O.P.:**

circa 1889-1892 **Other name:** *Ivy, Tree of Life* — there are too many patterns carrying these names as it is **Colors made:** white, blue and chartreuse opaque — rare in pink or butterscotch **Items made:** table set, salad bowl, preserves, salts, bowl. syrup jug, cruet, cracker jar (scarce) **Unreported:** sugar shaker, t.p. **Repro's:** none **Name by:** Orig. Mfr. name — *LEE VG*, plate 80 **Note:** The pattern is sometimes confused for the similar "sister" pattern, *Forget-Me-Not*. In fact, Peterson calls it that in his book on salt shakers. See the colored catalogue reprint on page 64.

CHALLINOR'S FORGET-ME-NOT (Figures 46-47)
Maker: Challinor & Taylor **Y.O.P.:** circa 1888, with continued U.S. Glass production after 1892 **Colors made:** opaque white, blue, pink, chartreuse and rare in butterscotch (Fig. 47) **Items made:** syrup, sugar shaker, cruet, toothpick, salts **Repro's:** none **Name by:** Brown's "Salt Dishes".

CHAMPION (Figure 48)
Maker: Primarily by McKee — also produced by Indiana Tumbler & Goblet **Y.O.P.:** from 1894 to as late as 1917, although colored production dates around 1900 **Colors made:** crystal, ruby & amber-stained, emerald green **Items made:** every shape imaginable **Name by:** Orig. Mfr. name (*Kamm 1*, pg. 106) **Note:** The syrup illustrated is quite scarce.

CHRYSANTHEMUM BASE SWIRL (Figures 49-50)
Maker: Indications are strong that this was made by Buckeye, although some sources credit Hobbs **Y.O.P.:** circa 1889 to 1895 **Colors**

(continued next page)

18

53
BULBOUS
(cranberry)

54
BULBOUS BASE
(green)

55
BULBOUS BASE
(cranberry)

56
9-PANEL MOLD
(green)

57
9-PANEL MOLD
(bittersweet)

58
SQUATTY
(blue)

59
TAPERED
(cranberry)

60
TAPERED
(blue)

61
WIDE-WAISTED
(cranberry)

62
COINSPOT & SWIRL
(blue)

(continued from previous page)

made: white, blue & cran. opales., sometimes satin finished   **Items made:** Listed in Book 2   **Repro's:** none   **Name by:** *Pet Sal,* pg. 24-U.

CHRYSANTHEMUM BASE SPECKLED (Figures 51-52)
Maker: Buckeye   **Y.O.P.:** same as above   **Colors:** crystal, blue & cran. speckled   **Items made:** same as the swirl variant   **Repro's:** none   **Name by:** Variation by author   **Note:** This is sometimes referred to incorrectly as "overshot" glass. The glass is actually covered with a coating of unvitrified sand, one of the earlier stages before it turns to glass. Overshot has a coating of bits of true glass.

COINSPOT (Figures 53-61)
Maker: This is almost impossible to report with complete authenticity, since the pattern was made for more than 20 years by every company which produced blown opalescent glass—but I will try.

Fig. 53: This one appears to be of later production. It is heavier than usual, but I am certain enough about its age to include it in this book. I would guess it is Jefferson glass, circa 1910. The top is not original.

Figs. 54-55: The *Bulbous Base* mold was originally made by Hobbs, but I doubt that the pieces shown here were made by them. The old Hobbs molds were acquired by Beaumont glass around 1895 and used for their own production, and it is to this company that I attribute these two scarce examples of *Coinspot*.

Figs. 56-57: The *Nine-Panel* mold undoubtedly was made by Northwood around 1905 (the syrup shown was advertised by Butler Brothers that year). The Oglebay Institute at Wheeling includes it with their examples of Hobbs ware, and it is possible that Northwood acquired

the molds when he purchased and reopened the closed-down Hobbs plant in 1902—but I doubt it. Much of their attribution is based on what local citizens told them and hearsay is a very dangerous form of historical research. This form of research is responsible for much of the confusion concerning Portland Glass.

Fig. 58: This little charmer is either Hobbs or Belmont glass, and dates quite early, circa 1885. The syrup shown is quite scarce in color, more often seen in white opalescent.

Fig. 59-60: The tapered shape was definitely made by Hobbs. The shape is the same as the non-opalescent *Inverted Thumbprint* variant, and their peach-blow sugar shaker. Made in a rare color of canary opalescent—which is an unusual color in which to find *Coinspot.*

Fig. 61: It is my sincerest hope to some day learn who made the wide-waisted sugar shaker mold. I strongly believe it is Northwood influenced, since it is the only shape that the *Spanish Lace* sugar shaker was made in—but exactly when? I feel it was during his Buckeye Glass association, and he retained usage of the patterns later at his own locations.

Coinspot was also made in the *Ring Neck* mold (Figs. 354, 377 in Book 2), and has been reproduced in cranberry by L. G. Wright. Table setting items (other than water sets) are rare—I have never seen a table set, or berry set.

COINSPOT & SWIRL (Figure 62)
Maker: Hobbs, at least originally   **Y.O.P.:** circa 1890   **Items made:** cruet, syrup jug only items reported   **Colors made:** white & blue opales—no amber or cranberry seen to date   **Repro's:** none   **Name by:** *Author*   **Other name:** *Swirl & Coin Dot* (Taylor).

63
COLUMBIA, BEAUMONT'S
(vaseline)

64
CONE
(blue satin)

65
CONE
(blue satin)

66
CONE
(yellow cased)

67
CONE, SQUATTY
(pink satin)

68
CONE, SQUATTY
(yellow satin)

69
CONE, SQUATTY
(lemon satin)

70
CONE
(blue cased)

71
CONE, SQUATTY
(blue cased)

72
CONE, SQUATTY
(lemon cased)

COLUMBIA, BEAUMONT'S (Figure 63)
Maker: Beaumont   **Y.O.P.:** circa 1898   **Colors made:** crystal & vaseline, usually with gold — ruby or amber-stained would be rare   **Items made:** Table, water & berry set, cruet, salts, syrup, high-standard compote, 8" & 10" plate, celery tray (which is also used as the tray for a cruet set), vases, t.p., jelly and celery vase. Many pieces are rare, especially the cruet in color   **Name by:** Original manufacturer's name (*Kamm 7,* plate 67)   **Other name:** *Beaumont's #100*   **Repro's:** none **Note:** There are other *Columbia* patterns, so this one should include the makers name for proper identification.

CONE (Figures 64-72)
Maker: Consolidated Lamp & Glass Co., primarily at Fostoria, Ohio **Y.O.P.:** circa 1894   **Other name:** the shorter version of the pattern is frequently called Half-Cone (see notes below)   **Colors made:** opaque,

cased & satin finish colors of white, green, pink, yellow and blue; also found rarely in cranberry and pigeon blood, with other experimental colors likely   **Pieces made:** table, water & berry set, sugar shaker (tall & short), syrup (tall & short), toothpick, cruet, celery vase, pickle caster insert, and salt shakers (tall & short)   **Name by:** Original Manufacturer's name (*Kamm 6,* plate 78)   **Repro's:** none   **IMPORTANT NOTE:** Peterson calls the squatty salt *Half-Cone,* which has caused a misconception that there are two different patterns. Since most pieces in this pattern have the *Half-Cone* characteristics (a plain upper portion with tight cones at the base), it is often labelled thus by dealers. The pattern should be heretofore referred to simply as *Cone.* The *Guttate* pattern salt shaker & syrup have both a tall & short size also, and yet this difference has caused no confusion to date. The so-called *Half-Cone* is nothing more than *Cone* with a slight change in the pattern to accommodate certain pieces of the table setting.

73
CORD DRAPERY
(chocolate)

74
CORD DRAPERY
(amber)

75
COREOPSIS, SHORT
(red satin)

76
CORSET & THUMBPRINT
(ruby-stain)

77
CORN
(turquoise opaque)

78
COSMOS
(decorated milk)

79
CREASED BALE
(pink opaque)

80
CREASED TEARDROP
(marble slag)

81
CREASED TEARDROP
(blue slag)

82
CREASED TEARDROP
(purple slag)

CORD DRAPERY (Figures 73-74)
Maker: Indiana Tumbler & Goblet **Y.O.P.:** from 1899 to 1903, with limited production later by Indiana Glass (in crystal) around 1910 **Name by:** *Kamm 1*, pg. 79 **Original Name:** *Indiana* **Colors made:** crystal, amber, chocolate, green & blue **Items made:** every shape imaginable **Repro's:** none to date (give them time).

COREOPSIS, SHORT (Figure 75)
Maker: Not absolutely certain—undoubtedly Kopp, possibly while with Consolidated Lamp & Glass, at Coraopolis, Pa. **Y.O.P.:** circa 1902 **Colors made:** glossy and satin finish decorated milk glass (extremely similar to *Cosmos* decoration) and rare in red satin with white decoration **Items made:** Table, water & berry set, syrup, cracker jar **Repro's:** none **Name by:** *Kamm 5*, pg. 52 **Note:** The butter dish in this pattern has a metal base. Sometimes the other items to the table set have applied metal rims and lids. The cracker jar also can have a glass lid. See page 52 for the taller syrup in this pattern.

CORSET & THUMBPRINT (Figure 76)
Maker: Unknown **Y.O.P.:** circa 1900 **Colors made:** clear & ruby-stained **Items made:** data not available at press time—further research pending **Repro's:** none **Name by:** *Author*.

CORN (Figure 77)
Maker: Undoubtedly Dithridge **Y.O.P.:** circa 1900 **Colors made:** opaque white, turquoise blue, green and custard yellow **Items made:** salt & sugar shaker **Repro's:** None **Name by:** *Pet Sal*, pg. 25-N.

COSMOS (Figure 78)
Maker: Known production by Consolidated, both at Fostoria, O. & later at Coraopolis, Pa.—likely acquisition of molds by another firm at a later date **Y.O.P.:** from 1894 to as late as 1915 **Colors made:** popular in the decorated milk glass (quite a bit available) **Items made:** water, table & berry set, syrup, condiment set, salts, mini. lamp, perfumes, pickle caster insert, trays **Repro's:** believe the miniature lamp has been re-made, but not decorated like the old **Undocumented:** cruet, toothpick & sugar shaker **IMPORTANT:** Do not be confused by lamps which appear to be *Cosmos* at first glance, but are actually similar patterns made by Fostoria Glass Co.

CREASED BALE (Figure 79)
Maker: Dithridge & Co. **Y.O.P.:** circa 1894 **Name by:** *Pet Sal*, pg. 25-X **Colors:** white, blue, pink & custard yellow **Items made:** syrup, t.p., & condiment set (salt, pepper & mustard on tray) **Repro's:** Peterson says the condiment set has been re-made, but I cannot confirm this.

CREASED TEARDROP (Figures 80-82)
Maker: Unknown **Y.O.P.:** circa 1900 **Colors:** all kinds of opaques & slags **Items made:** only sugar shaker reported to date **Name by:** Author **Repro's:** None **Note:** I have been told that the pieces illustrated could possibly be a large salt shaker, but they fit in well with a sugar shaker collection.

83
CRISS-CROSS
(rubina satin)

84
CURRIER & IVES
(amber)

85
DAISY & BUTTON
(sapphire blue)

86
DAISY & BUTTON
WITH CROSSBARS
(amber)

87
DAISY & BUTTON WITH
THUMBPRINT PANELS
(amber)

Daisy & Fern

88
APPLE BLOSSOM MOLD
(blue)

89
BULBOUS
(old reeded handle)

90
NORTHWOOD MOLD

91
W.VA. OPTIC MOLD
(blue)

92
WIDE-WAISTED
MOLD
(cranberry)

CRISS-CROSS (Figure 83)
Maker: Consolidated Lamp & Glass **Y.O.P.:** circa 1894 **Colors made:** white, cranberry & rubina opalescent, sometimes with a luscious art-glassy satin finish **Items made:** see listing in Book 2 **Name by:** *Author* **Repro's:** None **Note:** Production of this pattern was undoubtedly limited to the Fostoria, Ohio location, and to the years 1894-95. Certain items are extremely rare, including the syrup illustrated, the sugar shaker & the cruet.

CURRIER & IVES (Figure 84)
Maker: Bellaire Goblet Co., Findlay, Ohio with possible continued production after U.S. Glass absorption of the company **Y.O.P.:** circa 1890 (I have a blue wine with that year etched on it) **Colors:** crystal, amber and blue—extremely rare in canary **Items made:** almost everything, excluding a toothpick or cruet **Name by:** *LEE VG*, plt. 86 — the name is derived from the scenic tray to the water set **Repro's:** None.

DAISY & BUTTON (Figure 85)
Maker: Hobbs with possible continued production after U.S. Glass took it over **Y.O.P.:** circa 1890 **Colors:** crystal, sapphire blue, apple green, canary, amber **Items made:** both companies made a tremendous variety **Name by:** Popular Nomenclature **Repro's:** the syrup shown has not been reproduced. Contrary to opinion, this pattern is relatively safe if you know which patterns & items to avoid.

DAISY & BUTTON WITH CROSSBAR (Figure 86)
Maker: Richards & Hartley Flint Glass Co., Tarentum, Pa. **Y.O.P.:**

from 1888 up to, and perhaps following, their 1891 merger into the U.S. Glass Co. **Colors:** crystal, amber, blue & canary **Items made:** too numerous to list—Kamm says at least 45 items **Repro's:** I know of none **Note:** The syrup shown is scarce in color.

DAISY & BUTTON WITH THUMBPRINT (Figure 87)
Maker: Adams & Co., Pittsburgh **Y.O.P.:** circa 1888 with possible continued production by U.S. Glass **Colors:** crystal, amber, blue, amber-stained & blue-stained—these last two probably after 1892 **Items made:** a tremendous variety—see *Kamm 3*, pg. 73 for listing **Repro's:** Kamm says the goblet was reproduced during the 40's **NOTE:** The amber-stained pieces are sometimes confused for the popular Amberette pattern, which lacks the thumbprints in the panels. **Name by:** *Millard*.

DAISY & FERN (Figures 88-92)
Makers: Primarily by Northwood, but also by Buckeye, Jefferson & West Virginia Glass Companies **Y.O.P.:** from 1888 to as late as 1910 **Colors:** white, blue, cranberry and rare in green opales. **Items:** See listing Book 2—add a cruet & rose bowl to the list **Repro's:** massively reproduced by L. G. Wright for many years—avoid canary opalescent (they're still making that), beware of reeded handles, & avoid pieces with satin finish **Name by:** Popular Nomenclature **NOTES:** Fig. 88 is Northwood, circa 1895; Fig. 89 is probably Northwood, circa 1900 (one of the few old examples with a reeded handle); Fig. 90 is in Northwood's Royal Ivy mold; Fig. 91 is in West Virginia's *Optic* mold; Fig. 92 is either Buckeye or Northwood (probably this mold was used by both).

93
DAISY IN CRISS-CROSS
(cranberry)

94
DELTA
(amber)

95
DIAMOND SPEARHEAD
(green opal.)

96
DOUBLE THUMBPRINT BAND
(blue)

97
DRAPED GARLANDS
(ruby-stain)

98
EMPRESS
(emerald green)

99
ERIE TWIST
(glossy)

100
ERIE TWIST
(satiny)

101
FAMOUS
(apple green)

102
FEATHER
(emerald green)

DAISY IN CRISS-CROSS (Figure 93)
Maker: Beaumont Glass **Y.O.P.:** circa 1895 **Name by:** Taylor
Colors made: white, blue & cranberry opalescent **Items made:** only
syrup jug and water set (all rare) **Repro's:** none **Other name:**
Beaumont's Daisy.

DELTA (Figure 94)
Maker: Unknown **Y.O.P.:** circa 1895 **Colors:** crystal & amber only
colors seen to date **Items:** further research pending **Repro's:** None
Name by: *Author.*

DIAMOND SPEARHEAD (Figure 95)
Maker: After two books of guesses, this frustrating attribution can
now be made—Northwood Glass, Indiana, Pa. **Y.O.P.:** circa 1900
Colors made: crystal and opalescent colors of white, vaseline, green,
sapphire blue & cobalt blue **Items made:** see listing Book 2—add to
the tumblers and a high-standard compote **Repro's:** none **Other
name:** *Pressed Opal Top* (Boultinghouse) **Name by:** *Pet Sol.* pg. 159-
B **IMPORTANT:** Now that the Northwood attribution can be confirmed (see notes on page 9), this pattern will undoubtedly increase
rapidly in value.

DOUBLE THUMBPRINT BAND (Figure 96)
Maker: Unknown **Y.O.P.:** circa 1880 **Colors known:** crystal & blue
—vaseline, amber likely **Items made:** further research pending
Repro's: None **Name by:** Author **NOTE:** *Metz 2* shows a pattern
which resembles this, but it is listed only in a wine & decanter. On
the syrup shown here, the thumbprints are inverted at the top and
bulge out at the bottom.

DRAPED GARLAND (Figure 97)
Maker: Unknown at this time **Y.O.P.:** circa 1900 **Colors known:**

crystal and ruby-stained **Items:** undoubtedly a complete table service—Peterson shows a salt shaker, & shown here for the first time is
the syrup (research pending) **Repro's:** None **Name by:** *Pet Sal,*
pg. 159-Q **Note:** This is a very lovely pattern with a bright future.

EMPRESS (Figure 98)
Maker: Riverside **Y.O.P.:** circa 1898 **Colors:** crystal, emerald green
& extremely rare (experimental production) in amethyst **Items
made:** water & table set, berry set (2 shapes), t.p., cruet, syrup, jelly
compote, high-standard compotes, covered mustard, custard cup,
salt dip (hard to recognize), salt shaker, 2 oil lamps, nappies & plates,
rare breakfast creamer & sugar **Repro's:** None **Other Name:** *Double Arch* **NOTE:** The custard cup & the base to the mustard are
the same.

ERIE TWIST (Figures 99-100)
Maker: C. F. Monroe Company, Meriden, Conn. **Y.O.P.:** circa 1892
Items made: syrup, sugar shaker, salt shaker, tiny cream & sugar,
perhaps other **Colors:** luster & satin finish opal glass, often beautifully decorated—sometimes poorly decorated **Repro's:** none **Name
by:** *Pet Sal,* pg. 59 **NOTE:** The shape of this pattern was patented
in October, 1892 by Carl V. Helmschmeid, with the patent called a
design for a table vessel.

FAMOUS (Figure 101)
Maker: Cooperative Flint Glass Co. **Y.O.P.:** circa 1899 **Colors
made:** crystal, apple green & ruby-stained **Items made:** standard
table items **Repro's:** none **Name by:** Orig. mfr. name **Other name:**
Peterson calls it *Thumbprint Panel* **NOTE:** The syrup shown is
quite scrace.

(continued on page 92)

23

103	104	105	106	107
FERN, INVERTED (cranberry)	**FERN, INVERTED** (cranberry)	**FERN, OPALESCENT** (blue)	**FERN, OPALESCENT** (cranberry)	**FERNS & FLOWERS** (ivory opaque)

108	109	110	111	112
FINDLAY ONYX	**FINDLAY ONYX**	**FISHNET & POPPIES** (decorated milk)	**FLAT DIAMOND BOX** (ruby-stain)	**FLAT FLOWER** (blue opaque)

FERN, INVERTED (Figures 103-104)
Makers: The *Fern* design was made by at least 4 different companies (see listing Book 2) so it is difficult to provide attribution on the pieces shown here **Y.O.P.:** from circa 1890 to 1900 **Name by:** Author **Other names:** *Fern Sprays* **Colors:** blue & cranberry **Items made:** syrup, sugar shaker & cruet known in non-opalescent **Repro's:** None.

FERN, OPALESCENT (Figures 105-106)
Maker: See above **Name by:** Popular Nomenclature **Other names:** *Blue Opal* (Kamm), *Fern Sprays* (Har Op) **Colors:** white, blue & cran. opales. **Repro's:** None **Items made:** See Book 2—add a barber bottle to that listing.

FERNS & FLOWERS (Figure 107)
Maker: Uncertain **Y.O.P.:** circa 1895 **Name by:** *Author* **NOTE:** The lovely sugar shaker shown here is my first confrontation with this appealing pattern. It is in a lovely custard-like ivory, but no other colors have been reported. It would be indescribable in pink; turquoise and white would be more likely made. Further research pending.

FINDLAY ONYX (Figures 108-109)
Maker: Dalzell, Gilmore & Leighton, Findlay, O. **Y.O.P.:** 1889 **Colors made:** ivory onyx, rose onyx and cranberry onyx—perhaps other experimental colors exist, like black onyx **Items made:** table set, water set, berry set, syrup, sugar shaker, vase, salts, t.p. **Name:** Orig. Mfr. name **Repro's:** None.

FISHNET & POPPIES (Figure 110)
Maker: Unknown at this time **Y.O.P.:** circa 1895 **Colors made:**

decorated milk glass **Items made:** Only syrup **Repro's:** None **Name by:** Author.

FLAT DIAMOND BOX (Figure 111)
Maker: Fostoria Glass Co. **Y.O.P.:** circa 1893 **Colors:** crystal & ruby-stained **Items made:** standard-table service, with no toothpick or cruet reported to date **Repro's:** None **Name by:** *Kamm 3*, pg. 94 **Original Name:** *Germanic*.

FLAT FLOWER (Figure 112)
Maker: Undoubtedly Dithridge **Y.O.P.:** circa 1900 **Colors made:** white, turquoise blue & green opaque—would be rare in pink or custard yellow **Items made:** syrup, salt shaker (no sugar shaker seen as yet) **Repro's:** None **Name by:** *Pet Sal*, pg. 29-A.

FLORAL DIAMOND BAND (Fig. 113)
Maker: U.S. Glass Co., Factory "B" (Bryce Bros.) **Y.O.P.:** circa 1900 **Colors made:** crystal & blue seen to date **Items made:** Only the syrup **Repro's:** None **Name by:** Author **NOTES:** This syrup had me baffled for quite some time, until I spotted it in the old U.S. Glass catalogue I was given the opportunity to study. See pg. 83 for a reprint of this and other syrups illustrated in this rare catalogue.

FLORETTE (Figure 114)
Maker: Consolidated Lamp & Glass **Y.O.P.:** from 1894 to 1900 **Colors made:** almost every opaque color imaginable—cased, opaque & satin finish colors of white, pink, crystal, blue, green, yellow, pidgeon blood, cranberry, and a peachblow-colored pink blending with white **Items made:** table, water & berry set, syrup, sugar shaker,

(continued next page)

113	114	115	116	117
FLORAL DIAMOND BAND (blue)	**FLORETTE** (pink satin)	**FLOWER MOLD** (blue)	**FLOWERED SCROLL** (amber-stain)	**FRANCES WARE SWIRL**

118	119	120	121	122
GARGOYLE (milk)	**GENEVA** (ivory)	**GLOBULE** (red satin)	**GONTERMAN SWIRL** (amber top)	**GONTERMAN SWIRL** (blue top)

(continued from previous page)

syrup, t.p., salts, mustard, condiment set, cracker jars (metal or glass lids), celery vase, cruet, powder jar, bride's bowl, mini. lamp, boudoir lamp (with silk or glass shade)   **Repro's:** cracker jar has been well-produced recently   **Note:** The powder jar is the spooner mold with a fancy metal lid   **Name by:** Orig. Mfr. name — *Kamm 6.* plt. 87.

FLOWER MOLD (Figures 115 & 359)
Maker: Beaumont Glass   **Y.O.P.:** circa 1895   **Colors made:** cranberry, blue & emerald green   **Items made:** salt, sugar shaker, syrup   **Repro's:** None   **Name by:** *Taylor*   **NOTE:** Obviously had limited production. See ad reprint in color, page 61.

FLOWERED SCROLL (Figure 116)
Maker: Geo. Duncan Sons & Co.   **Y.O.P.:** 1893   **Colors made:** crystal & amber-stained   **Items made:** a considerable table service, although no cruet or toothpick has been reported   **Repro's:** None   **Name by:** *Metz #2533*   **Note:** The syrup shown here is very hard to find; this was Duncan's #2000 pattern.

FRANCES WARE SWIRL (Figure 117)
Maker: Hobbs   **Y.O.P.:** from 1885 to 1892   **Colors made:** clear or frosted with amber-stained rim at top—seldom found with no color at all (see Fig. 300)   **Items made:** water, table & berry set, t.p., syrup, sugar shaker, celery vase, celery tray, pickle tray, salt shaker, mustard   **Repro's:** None   **Name by:** *Pet Sal*, pg. 162-B.

GARGOYLE (Figure 118)
Maker: Gillinder & Sons   **Y.O.P.:** circa 1905   **Colors made:** only milk white seen to date—would be rare in color or decorated   **Items made:**

salt shaker, sugar shaker, cologne bottle   **Repro's:** none   **Name by:** *Millard.*

GENEVA (Figure 119)
Maker: Northwood Glass   **Y.O.P.:** advertised in 1901 by Montgomery Wards   **Colors made:** crystal, emerald green, ivory opaque (similar to custard, and collected as such), and scarce in chocolate glass   **Items made:** Water, table & berry set (the latter in round or oval shape), t.p., salt, syrup, cruet   **Repro's:** none   **Name by:** Original name as advertised in Wards catalogue (see *Kamm 6*, plt. 6).

GLOBULE (Figure 120)
Maker: Lancaster Glass Works, Lancaster, Ohio   **Y.O.P.:** advertised in 1901 (see reprint on page 85)   **Colors made:** milk glass and rare in red satin   **Items made:** salt shaker & syrup known to date   **Repro's:** None   **Name by:** *Warman's MGA*   **NOTE:** The unfortunate name given this pattern does little to describe its beauty. Discovering the maker of this syrup (I had previously assumed it was Kopp glass— the "king" of red satin) was a distinct thrill.

GONTERMAN SWIRL (Figures 121-122)
Maker: Probably Hobbs, as reported in Books 1 & 2   **Y.O.P.:** circa 1886   **Colors made:** amber or blue top, frosted or opalescent base   **Items made:** see listing Book 2—add a finger bowl to that listing.   **Repro's:** none   **Name by:** *Author*   **Note:** It has just been brought to my attention that the sugar lid on the *Beatty Swirl* pattern and this one are almost identical. The explanation for this is simple—famed glass-maker William Leighton, Jr. was associated with both Hobbs and later Beatty Glass, and perhaps was directly involved in the design of these two patterns.

25

123	124	125	126	127
GRAPE & LEAF (green cased)	**GUTTATE** (raspberry satin)	**GUTTATE** (peach bloom)	**GUTTATE** (pink satin)	**GUTTATE** (pink satin)

128	129	130	131	132
GUTTATE (cranberry)	**GUTTATE, SQUATTY** (cranberry)	**GUTTATE, SQUATTY** (pink cased)	**HEXAGON BLOCK** (ruby-stain)	**HER MAJESTY** (decorated cranberry)

GRAPE & LEAF (Figure 123)
Maker: Possibly Northwood, although only speculative **Y.O.P.:** circa 1905 **Colors made:** opaque colors of white, blue & green—also cased colors. The syrup was also offered in crystal with white opalescent *Coinspots* in a 1905 Sears, Roebuck catalogue **Items made:** salt, cruet & syrup known **Repro's:** none **Name by:** *Warman MGA* **ATTRIBUTION NOTES:** The Northwood label is due to color, pattern and other characteristics. The cased green is almost identical to *Quilted Phlox* which I had previously thought was Kopp, but now feel is Northwood.

GUTTATE (Figures 124-130)
Maker: Consolidated Lamp & Glass, Fostoria, Ohio **Y.O.P.:** circa 1894 **Colors made:** opaque, cased & satin finish colors of white, pink, green and turquoise blue—also made in deep cranberry, sometimes cased inside with a white lining. Figure 124 is this color, with a rare satiny finish **Items made:** table, water & berry set, t.p., salt shakers (short & tall), sugar shaker, syrup, celery, cruet, mustard **Repro's:**

new tumblers on the market in satin finish colors (including yellow) **Name by:** *Millard* **Notes:** The base to the butter dish in this pattern is a frosted glass flattened bowl. The syrup is found in both a tall and squatty version.

HEXAGON BLOCK (Figure 131)
Maker: Hobbs Glass Co. **Y.O.P.:** circa 1889, with production continued after U.S. Glass takeover in 1891 **Colors made:** crystal, ruby and amber-stained **Items made:** Considerable table service—no toothpick or cruet known **Repro's:** none **Name by:** *PET SAL*, pg. 30-T **Original name:** Hobbs #330.

HER MAJESTY (Figure 132)
Maker: Uncertain, although probably from one of the New England glass firms **Y.O.P.:** circa 1890 **Colors:** cranberry, blue, amberina, others **Repro's:** Not with the quality decoration shown on Fig. 132 **Name by:** *Author* **Note:** The top is a 2-piece pewter apparatus.

133	134	135	136	137
HERCULES PILLAR (sapphire blue)	**HOBB'S SATINA SWIRL** (cranberry satin)	**HOBB'S SATINA SWIRL** (amber satin)	**HOBNAIL** (blue)	**HOBNAIL** (cranberry)

Hobnail by Hobbs

138	139	140	141	142
(Frances Ware)	(Unfrosted Frances Ware)	(Rubina)	(Rubina Opales.)	(Rubina Verde)

HERCULES PILLAR (Figure 133)
Maker: Hobbs, Brockunier **Y.O.P.:** circa 1875—this one is quite early, although the colored production may have been a reissue of the 90's **Colors made:** crystal, amber, blue & apple green—canary would be scarce **Items made:** Not known by this writer (goblet & syrup only items documented to date) **Repro's:** none **Name by:** *Metz & Millard*.

HOBB'S SATINA SWIRL (Figures 134-135)
Maker: Hobbs, Brockunier & Co. **Y.O.P.:** circa 1885 **Colors made:** camphor, blue, lemon yellow, cranberry, and amber satin **Items made:** table, water & berry set, cruet (often referred to as a "Swans-bill" cruet), salt & pepper, celery vase, syrup jug, fairy lamp shades **Repro's:** none **Name by:** see *LEE VG*, plate 246 **Note:** as old and as lovely as this glass is, it has not yet received the attention and collectibility it so richly deserves.

HOBNAIL, HOBBS' (Figure 136-142)
Maker: Hobbs **Y.O.P.:** from circa 1885 to its closing in 1892 (the molds were re-issued in a few limited items by Beaumont & North-wood) **Colors made:** crystal, cranberry, sapphire blue, rubina, amberina, rubina verde (Fig. 142), vaseline (with all of these also found with opalescent hobs), the popular *Frances Ware*, and solid frosted glass colors of crystal, blue, amber **Items made:** water, table & berry set, cruet, syrup, toothpick (in a few colors), finger bowl (or waste), celery vase, pitchers of several sizes, bride's bowl, barber's bottle, lamps of all sizes, water tray **Repro's:** the only new items which can fool you are the reproduction barber bottle and the new tumblers which have just come out **Name by:** Popular Nomenclature **Note:** See the cruet (Fig. 431) in the exciting and rare frosted rubina color—extremely popular & highly collectible. The rubina verde syrup shown above is even more rare. I have also seen Hobbs' hobnail in cased glass colors of white and an unusual ice green.

27

143 HOBNAIL, PRESSED (green)	144 HOBNAIL, PRESSED (blue)	145 HOLLY AMBER	146 HORSESHOE (amber)	147 HONEYCOMB, OPALES. (blue)	148 HOURGLASS MOLD (vaseline etched)

149 INSIDE RIBBED (blue)	150 INVERTED THUMBPRINT (baby)	151 IVT (bulbous)	152 IVT (decorated)	153 IVT (pinched base)

HOBNAIL, PRESSED (Figures 143-144)
Maker: U.S. Glass Factory "C" (Columbia Glass Co.) **Y.O.P.:** the sugar shakers shown here were made as early as 1890 to as late as 1930 **Colors made:** crystal, amber, blue, deep emerald green **Name by:** Popular nomenclature **Repro's:** production so continuous it is hard to tell — I know of none being made today **NOTE:** See ad reprint pg. 68.

HOLLY AMBER (Figure 145)
Maker: Indiana Tumbler & Goblet Co., Greentown, Ind. **Y.O.P.:** 1903, with extremely limited production **Colors made:** crystal (referred to as *Holly Clear*), and in the highly popular amber with opalescence **Items made:** a complete table set, several unusual items like a toothpick on a pedestal, covered compotes, vases, etc. **Repro's:** new toothpicks in all kinds of colors, including those originally made, a new tumbler **Name by:** HERR, pg. 28-30 **Original name:** *Golden Agate* **Note:** I cannot fully express my appreciation for the trust the owners of this syrup had in me to allow its removal from their home for inclusion in this book. It is without doubt the most valuable piece shown in this book.

HORSESHOE (Figure 146)
Maker: Unknown, although the piece shown was patented in January 1900, and was originally used for marketing snuff **Colors made:** crystal and amber **Items made:** a small size (found in salt shaker collections) and a large size (seen in sugar shaker collections) **Repro's:** none **Name by:** *Horseshoe, Big* by Pet Sal, pg. 31-K.

HONEYCOMB, OPALESCENT (Figure 147)
Maker: Undoubtedly Hobbs' **Y.O.P.:** circa 1890 **Colors made:** white,

blue & cranberry opales. **Items made:** water set, syrup jug, cracker jar **Repro's:** None **Other name:** Taylor calls this *Bulbous Spot Resist* **Name by:** *Author* **Notes:** The pattern is very similar in concept to *Opalescent Windows* and *Polka Dot*, except a close study of Fig. 147 reveals that the spots are six-side. A little time should be taken to study these three patterns and learn the differences.

HOURGLASS MOLD (Figure 148)
Maker: unknown, although the silver-plated lid & handle are signed Tufts **Y.O.P.:** circa 1895 **Colors made:** only vaseline etched piece illustrated has been seen to date **Items made:** this is not pattern glass — it is included only because it will prove interesting to syrup collectors **Name by:** *Author.*

INSIDE RIBBED (Figure 149)
Maker: Beaumont seems the likely choice here **Y.O.P.:** circa 1900 **Colors made:** crystal, canary, emerald green, blue **Items made:** I previously thought this was the syrup to Kamm's "Inside Ribbing," but the syrup here is mold blown, not pressed **Repro's:** none **Name by:** *Taylor*, plate #11.

INVERTED THUMBPRINT (Figures 150-158)
Maker: Most of this blown pattern was made by Hobbs, although additional production was likely by Northwood, Belmont, Duncan and possibly the New England glass companies **Y.O.P.:** from 1885 to 1900 **Colors made:** cranberry, blue, apple green, rubina, amberina, rubina verde — with opalescent dots the pattern becomes *Coinspot* **Items made:** See *LEE VG*, plate 94 for a wide variety **Name by:** Popular nomenclature **Note:** See pgs. 67 & 75 for ad reprints featuring this pattern.

154	155	156	157	158
IVT (rubina)	**IVT** (tapered)	**IVT** (tapered)	**IVT** (amberina)	**IVT** (tapered)

159	160	161	162	163
JEWELLED HEART	**JEWELLED HEART**	**JEWELLED HEART** (apple green)	**JEWELLED HEART** (apple green)	**KING'S #500** (cobalt)

INVERTED THUMBPRINT (Figures 150-158)
See notes concerning pattern on previous page.

JEWELLED HEART (Figures 159-162)
Maker: Northwood Glass, Indiana, Pa. **Y.O.P.:** circa 1900, with production possibly continued after Dugan Glass took over **Items made:** water, table & berry set, cruet & cruet set (see Figure   ), toothpick, syrup jug, sugar shaker, salt shaker, tray to cruet set (or plate), large chop plate **Colors made:** crystal, apple green & blue — opalescent white, green & blue — also scarce in carnival marigold **Reproductions:** new toothpicks, goblets and a new breakfast-size creamer & covered sugar in all colors **Name by:** Kamm 5, pg. 41 **IMPORTANT NOTE:** Up to now the Northwood attribution had been nothing but conjecture. Now this attribution can be positively confirmed due to the shards found in the Indiana, Pa. diggings.

KING'S #500 (Figure 163)
Maker: The King Glass Co., Pittsburgh, Pa. **Y.O.P.:** circa 1890 to 1900, the later production after the U.S. Glass absorption. **Colors made:** crystal and a beautiful deep cobalt blue (often with gold) **Items made:** So many, it is impossible to list them here — these include a rare oil lamp, cruet, salt shakers (very rare) **Name by:** Kamm 8, pg. 72 **Other name:** Parrot (see notes) **Note:** The cobalt blue color shown here is typical of several other U.S. Glass patterns, including *Broken Column, Bead & Scroll* and even occasional pieces of *King's Crown.* The "Parrot" label is a massive misconception among collectors. Kamm was referring to a figural parrot syrup in an accompanying ad by Dalzel, Gilmore & Leighton, not *King's 500.*

164
LEAF, DROOPING
(decorated milk)

165
LEAF MOLD
(cased cranberry spatter)

166
LEAF MOLD

167
LEAF MOLD
(vaseline satin spatter)

168
LEAF MOLD
(vaseline spatter)

169
LEAF MOLD
(rubina stripe)

170
LEAF MOLD
(blue satin)

171
LEAF MOLD
(camphor satin)

172
LEAF MOLD
(lime green)

173
LEAF & FLOWER
(amber-stain satin)

LEAF DROOPING (Figure 164)
Maker: Unknown   **Y.O.P.:** circa 1900   **Notes:** Only the syrup & salt shaker have been documented to date   **Name:** *Pet Sal,* pg. 165-B.

LEAF MOLD (Figures 165-172)
Maker: My research continues into this pattern's origins, but no ad or catalogue has yet been found to provide the necessary dating for positive attribution. *Leaf Mold* is either Northwood or Hobbs or both (Northwood reissued old Hobbs' molds when he bought their long-idle plant)   **Y.O.P.:** circa 1890   **Colors made:** see listing Book 2   **Items made:** see listing Book 2 — add a perfume bottle & rose bowl to the list   **Repro's:** None   **Name by:** *Taylor,* plate #14   **NOTES:** See Book 1

and 2 for other information concerning this pattern which has risen from virtual anonymity in 1974 to a fast-growing peak of popularity in 1975. Its future looks even brighter!

LEAF & FLOWER (Figure 173)
Maker: Hobbs, Brockunier   **Y.O.P.:** circa 1888 to 1892   **Colors made:** crystal, frosted & clear, amber-stained, frosted & amber-stained   **Items made:** Table set, water set, berry set, syrup, salt shaker, finger bowl (waste bowl), celery vase, celery basket, and Lee lists a caster set which I have never witnessed to date.   **Repro's:** none   **Name by:** *LEE VG,* plate 50   **NOTE:** No toothpick or cruet was originally made.

174
LEAF UMBRELLA
(cranberry)

175
LEAF UMBRELLA
(mauve)

176
LEAF UMBRELLA
(lemon)

177
LEAF UMBRELLA
(blue satin)

178
LEAF UMBRELLA
(cranberry spatter)

179
LEANING PILLARS

180
LEANING PILLARS

181
LEANING PILLARS

182
LITTLE SHRIMP
(ivory)

183
LITTLE SHRIMP
(turquoise blue)

184
LITTLE SHRIMP
(decorated satin)

LEAF UMBRELLA (Figures 174-178)
Maker: Northwood at Martin's Ferry **Y.O.P.:** circa 1890 **Colors made:** cranberry, and cased colors of mauve (pink), blue, yellow and a lovely cranberry spatter — the blue & yellow are sometimes satin-finished **Items made:** table set (the butter looks like a covered candy bowl), water set, cracker jar, berry set, syrup, sugar shaker, tooth-pick, celery vase, finger bowl, cruet, salt shaker, covered powder jar with metal lid **Name by:** *Pet Sal*, pg. 32-S **Repro's:** None **NOTE:** This was Northwood's #263 Ware, and production was undoubtedly limited — certain pieces are extremely scarce.

LEANING PILLARS (Figures 179-181)
Maker: Unknown **Y.O.P.:** circa 1895 **Colors made:** crystal, amber and a pale blue **Items made:** Only syrup & sugar shaker documented to date — other forms seem likely **Repro's:** none **Name by:** *Author*.

LITTLE SHRIMP (Figures 182-184)
Maker: Undoubtedly Dithridge **Y.O.P.:** circa 1895 **Colors made:** white, pink, turquoise blue, custard and decorated satin glass **Items made:** sugar shaker & salt shaker **Repro's:** None **Name by:** *PET SAL*, pg. 39-L.

31

185
MAIZE, LIBBEY'S
(custard color)

186
MAJESTIC
(ruby-stain)

187
MANY LOBES
(custard)

188
MANY LOBES
(white satin)

189
MANY LOBES
(turquoise)

190
MARIO
(amber-stain)

191
MAYFLOWER
(blue opaque)

192
MEDALLION SPRIG

193
MEDALLION SPRIG

194
MEDALLION SPRIG
(rubina)

195
MEDALLION SPRIG
(amber)

MAIZE, LIBBEY'S (Figure 185) (See also Figure 361)
Maker: Primarily by W. L. Libbey & Sons, Toledo, Ohio—although I have heard ridiculous reports that pieces with the blue decorated leaves were from the original New England Glass Co.; see notes below **Y.O.P.:** beginning in 1889 **Colors made:** decorated crystal, milk and ivory opal—the latter frequently referred to as the "custard" color **Decoration:** the crystal is decorated with an iridescent coating which has lead many collectors into calling it carnival glass — the opaque pieces can be found with yellow, green, blue, brown or rust colored leaves **Repro's:** several pieces have appeared recently in cased glass colors and none of these should fool anyone—they are not old!! **Name by:** Original mfr. name **Notes:** The patent for the Maize pattern was issued in 1889, whereas the New England Glass Co. closed its doors the previous year. It seems unlikely that they ever produced Maize at their Massachusetts plant location.

MAJESTIC (Figure 186)
Maker: McKee & Brothers, while at their Pittsburgh location **Y.O.P.:** circa 1893 **Colors made:** crystal, ruby-stained and rare in green **Items made:** every shape imaginable **Repro's:** None **Name by:** Orig. Mfr. name (see *Kamm 6*, plt. 70).

MANY LOBES (Figures 187-189)
Maker: Unknown, although Dithridge is the likely suspect **Y.O.P.:** circa 1900 **Colors made:** white, custard, pink, turquoise & blue opaque—also decorated satin glass **Items made:** only sugar shaker seen to date **Repro's:** none **Name by:** *Author.*

MARIO (Figure 190)
Maker: Originally by Hobb's, with later re-issue by U.S. Glass Co. **Y.O.P.:** circa 1890-1895 **Colors made:** crystal, ruby-stained & amber-stained **Items made:** Complete table set, and also a barber bottle, water bottle & salt shaker **Unreported items:** toothpick & cruet **Repro's:** none **Name by:** *LEE VG*, plate 43 **NOTE:** Lee reports that this pattern was Duncan's #341, although Revi shows an old catalogue reprint which shows it was Hobbs #341 instead. See reprint on page 69, this book.

MAYFLOWER (Figure 191)
Maker: Fostoria Glass Co., Moundsville, W. Va. **Y.O.P.:** circa 1900 **Colors made:** opaque white and blue known **Items made:** syrup, lamps, possibly others **Repro's:** None **Name by:** Orig. Mfr. name, illustrated in a 1901 catalogue, a portion of which is reprinted on page 60.

MEDALLION SPRIG (Figures 192-195)
Maker: West Virginia Glass Co. **Y.O.P.:** circa 1894 **Colors made:** crystal, rubina, amber (rare), and graduating blue, amethyst & green to clear **Items made:** table set, water set, berry set, toothpick, sugar shaker, cruet, salt shaker, syrup jug, finger bowl **Repro's:** None **Name by:** *PET SAL*, pg. 33-S **Other name:** *Stylistic Leaf* (Boultinghouse) **NOTES:** See ad reprint in Book 1, page 57.

196
MELLIGO
(blue opaque)

197
MELLIGO
(amber decorated)

198
MELLIGO
(emerald green)

199
MILLARD
(ruby-stain)

200
MINNESOTA
(ruby-stain)

201
NETTED OAK
(decorated milk)

202
NETTED OAK
(decorated milk)

203
NETTED OAK
(amethyst)

204
NINE-PANEL
(blue)

205
NINE-PANEL
(blue)

MELLIGO (Figures 196-198)
Maker: Consolidated Lamp & Glass **Y.O.P.:** circa 1895 **Colors made:** Opaque colors of white, blue and possibly pink & pale green — crystal colors of green, blue and amber, sometimes decorated poorly **Items made:** I have only seen sugar shakers & syrups in this one **Repro's:** None **Name by:** *Author* **Note:** Attribution is based on a shard in this pattern which appears on the back of Melvin Murray's book on Fostoria, Ohio glass. Previously unlisted pattern.

MILLARD (Figure 199)
Maker: U.S. Glass Co. **Y.O.P.:** circa 1895 **Colors made:** crystal, ruby-stained & amber-stained, sometimes etched **Items made:** complete set **Repro's:** none **Name by:** *LEE VG*, plt. 52 **Other name:** *Fan & Flute* (Kamm) **NOTE:** This was U.S. Glass #15016 pattern, and is identical in shape (not pattern) to their *Kentucky* pattern.

MINNESOTA (Figure 200)
Maker: U.S. Glass Co. **Y.O.P.:** circa 1898 **Colors made:** crystal primarily — scarce in ruby-stained and emerald green **Items made:** complete table set **Repro's:** None **Name by:** Orig. Mfr. name — part of the state's series **NOTE:** *Minnesota* was U.S. Glass #15055 pattern.

NETTED OAK (Figure 201-203)
Maker: Northwood Glass Co. **Y.O.P.:** circa 1895 to 1905 **Colors made:** poorly decorated milk glass, especially when goofus gold was used — also made in crystal, apple green, and rare in amethyst or blue **Items made:** water set, table set, berry set, syrup, sugar shaker, cruet — no toothpick or salt shaker have been reported to date **Repro's:** none **Name by:** popular nomenclature — also called *Acorn* (Belknap) and sometimes *Netted Royal Oak* **INTERESTING NOTE:** It is noteworthy here to mention that the decoration on the milk glass pieces is uncannily similar to the decoration on *Panelled Sprig* (Figure 358) and some pieces of *Quilted Phlox*. Also, all three of these patterns can be found in identical colors. *Presnick 2*, plate 235 reports a piece in blue iridescent.

NINE-PANEL (Figure 204-205)
Maker: Probably Northwood **Y.O.P.:** circa 1903-1905 **Colors made:** crystal, amethyst, apple green & blue — the mold was also used for variants in the *Coinspot & Blown Twist* patterns **Items made:** sugar shaker & syrup, water pitcher (with a round tumbler) **Repro's:** yes (thick) **Name by:** *Taylor*, plt. 10.

206
O'HARA'S DIAMOND
(ruby-stain)

207
O'HARA'S DIAMOND
(ruby-stain)

208
OPEN-HEART ARCHES
(cobalt decorated)

209
OPTIC, HOBB'S
(rubina)

210
OPTIC, HOBB'S
(rubina, etched)

211
PANELLED DAISY
(amber)

212
PANELLED DAISY
(blue)

213
PANELLED SPRIG
(amethyst)

214
PANELLED SPRIG
(blue speckled)

215
PANELLED SPRIG
(cranberry)

216
PANELLED SPRIG
(apple green)

O'HARA DIAMOND (Figures 206-207)
Maker: O'Hara Glass Company, Pittsburgh, with production continued by the U.S. Glass Co. **Y.O.P.:** 1885 to 1895 **Colors made:** crystal & ruby-stained **Items made:** practically everything except a toothpick holder **Repro's:** None **Name by:** Kamm 5, pg. 46 **Other name:** Earlier it was called *Sawtooth & Star* by *LEE VG*, plate 47.

OPEN-HEART ARCHES (Figure 208)
Maker: Either Consolidated or Pittsburgh Lamp **Y.O.P.:** circa 1905 **Items made:** table set, berry set, celery vase, syrup, pickle caster, jam jar, cracker jar **Colors made:** Cobalt blue (illus.), white satin decorated, and red satin **Repro's:** None **Name by:** *Author* **IMPORTANT:** I have often heard the white satin version of this pattern referred to as *Mt. Washington Lusterless.* This pattern was **not** made by them—it was made by Kopp while associated with Consolidated or perhaps shortly after the formation of the Pittsburgh Lamp, Brass & Glass Co. in 1905. All pieces to this pattern have metal rims and/or lids.

OPTIC, HOBB'S (Figures 209-210)
Maker: Hobbs, Brockunier & Co. **Y.O.P.:** circa 1888 **Colors made:** I have only seen this in rubina to date **Items made:** salt shaker, toothpick (in *Ring-Neck* mold), syrup, sugar shaker, cracker jar, berry set, water set, cruet, celery and a table set would be rare **Repro's:** None **Name by:** Orig. Mfr. Name (see *Revi*, pg. 190) **IMPORTANT NOTE:** The pattern can sometimes be found with delicate etchwork. Hobbs used their *Optic* mold on several other lines, including *Prima Donna*, and spatter glass items.

PANELLED DAISY (Figures 211-212)
Maker: Bryce Brothers, with continued production after U.S. Glass Company absorbed the factory **Y.O.P.:** circa 1889-1893 **Colors made:** crystal, milk glass, amber & blue **Items made:** complete table service, with the syrup in color an extreme rarity **Repro's:** none **Name by:** *LEE EAPG*, plate 95 **Original Name:** *Brazil* **NOTE:** See syrup on page 78.

PANELLED SPRIG (Figures 213-216)
Maker: Shards of this pattern have been unearthed at Northwood's Indiana, Pa. factory site—thus my conclusions from Book 1 & 2 are probably incorrect **Y.O.P.:** from 1895 to 1905 **Colors made:** crystal, rubina, cranberry, apple green, amethyst, blue, and clear with opalescent lattice-design—very rare with the speckled finish (Fig. 214) **Items made:** table set, water set, berry set, cruet (reproduced), syrup, sugar shaker, toothpick (see Book 1), celery vase, pickle caster insert, salt shaker, jam jar (metal rim & top) **Repro's:** new cruets & salt shakers by Wright **Name by:** *Author* **Note:** See milk glass version of this pattern on pg. 49 (#358).

PANELLED TEARDROP (Figures 217-218)
Maker: Tarentum Glass Co. **Y.O.P.:** circa 1908 **Colors made:** true custard glass and in pea-green opaque (often called green custard) **Items made:** sugar shaker, and condiment set (salt, pepper & mustard on a tray) **Repro:** none **Name by:** *PET SAL*, pg. 41-P **NOTES:** This pattern appears to be much later ware, similar to McKee's late custard, but it ,is not. The attribution is based on the exact color matchup to Tarentum's other colors.

(continued on next page)

34

| 218 PANELLED TEARDROP (custard) | 217 PANELLED TEARDROP (green custard) | 219 PANSY, BULGE-BOTTOM (decorated milk) | 220 PARIAN SWIRL (green opaque) | 221 PARIAN SWIRL (cranberry, glossy) | 222 PARIAN SWIRL (blue satin) |

| 223 PEARLY GATES (blue opaque) | 224 PEARLY PANELS (green opaque) | 225 PILGRIM BOTTLE (vaseline) | 226 PETTICOAT (vaseline) | 227 POINSETTIA, OPALES. (blue) |

(continued from previous page)

PANSY, BULGE BOTTOM (Figure 219)
Maker: Dithridge   **Y.O.P.:** circa 1895   **Colors made:** only decorated milk glass seen to date   **Items made:** syrup, salt shaker   **Repro's:** None   **Name by:** Peterson (Salts) calls this *Bulge Bottom*, but the huge pansies rate inclusion in the pattern name.

PARIAN SWIRL (Figures 220-222)
Maker: Northwood   **Y.O.P.:** advertised by Montgomery Wards in 1894 as "Parian Ruby"   **Colors made:** satin camphor, frosted & glossy cranberry, blue satin, and Figure 220 reveals a most unusual green opaque   **Items made:** table set, water set, berry set, toothpick, syrup, sugar shaker, night lamp, cruet, salt & pepper   **Repro's:** none   **Name by:** *Author*   **NOTE:** All pieces to this pattern are shaped exactly like corresponding pieces of Royal Ivy. The pattern is sometimes beautifully enamel-decorated.

PEARLY GATES (Figure 223)
Maker: Uncertain   **Y.O.P.:** circa 1895   **Colors made:** white & blue opaque—pink opaque would be too beautiful to imagine   **Items made:** the charming sugar shaker shown here is the only item I have had reported to me   **Repro's:** none   **Name by:** *Author.*

PEARLY PANELS (Figure 224)
Maker: Fostoria Glass Co.   **Y.O.P.:** circa 1902   **Colors made:** white, blue and green opaque known   **Items made:** only syrup seen to date   **Repro's:** none   **Name by:** Author   **IMPORTANT:** A very similar syrup (Figure 362) is shown in the ad reprint on page 60. They are identical except for the flower in the center.

PILGRIM BOTTLE (Figure 225)
Maker: Previously unattributed—this was made by Belmont Glass Co., at Bellaire, Ohio   **Y.O.P.:** circa 1882   **Colors made:** crystal, amber, blue and vaseline   **Items made:** table set, cruet, salt shaker, syrup   **Repro's:** none   **Name by:** *Kamm 6*, pg. 21   **NOTE:** Attribution is based on an old Belmont catalogue I was privileged in studying.

PETTICOAT (Figure 226)
Maker: Definitely Riverside Glass Co., while a part of the National Glass Company   **Y.O.P.:** circa 1901   **Colors made:** crystal and vaseline   **Items made:** water set, table set, berry set, cruet, toothpick, syrup, hat-shaped novelties, salt shaker, any other shape would be rare   **Repro's:** none   **Name by:** *PET SAL*, pg. 35-J   **NOTE:** See Book 1 for more information concerning this pattern.

POINSETTIA, OPALESCENT (Figure 227)
Maker: Hobbs, Brockunier with additional production by Northwood   **Y.O.P.:** from 1890 to 1910   **Colors made:** white, blue, cranberry and canary opalescent — later production in marigold carnival   **Items made:** water set (3 different shape pitchers), syrup jug (see page 52), sugar shaker, and a bride's bowl (seen with a cobalt blue applied edge)   **Repro's:** none   **Name by:** Popular nomenclature   **Other name:** *Big Daisy* (Taylor)   **NOTES:** shards of this pattern have been unearthed at the old Hobbs plant site in Wheeling, W. Va. Both Hobbs & Northwood used this plant, and it is difficult to determine which company made which pieces (except for the carnival).

228
POLKA DOT
(cranberry)

229
POLKA DOT
(bulbous)

230
POLKA DOT
(blue)

231
POLKA DOT
(cranberry)

232
PORTLY PANELS
(blue)

233
PRESSED DIAMOND
(vaseline)

234
PRESSED OCTAGON
(amber decorated)

235
PRETTY PANELS
(amber)

236
PRIMA DONNA
(cranberry-spatter)
(vasa murrhina)

237
PRISCILLA, FOSTORIA'S
(emerald green)

POLKA DOT (Figures 228-231)

Maker: Production is now known to have been undertaken at North-wood's Indiana, Pa. factory site (shards were unearthed there)—additional production by the West Virginia Glass Co. in their "Optic" mold (see Book 1, Fig. 201) **Y.O.P.:** circa 1894 to 1900 **Colors made:** white, blue & cranberry opalescent **Items made:** not certain about the water set yet—the ones I've seen looked suspicious (Wright reproduces this); other items include the syrups & sugar shakers (2 different shapes for each), salt shaker, toothpick holder **Repro's:** See book 2, pg. 91 (and illustrations) **Name by:** *PET SAL*, pg. 35-S.

PORTLY PANELS (Figure 232)

Maker: Unknown **Y.O.P.:** circa 1895 **Colors made:** I have only seen the blue color illustrated, although others are more than likely **Items made:** sugar shaker & syrup **Repro's:** none **Name by:** *Author*

PRESSED DIAMOND (Figure 233)

Maker: Central Glass Co., Wheeling **Y.O.P.:** circa 1885 (their #775 pattern) **Colors made:** crystal, amber, canary, blue and rare in apple green **Items made:** complete table service—the syrup is very rare (no toothpick was made) **Repro's:** none **Name by:** *LEE VG*, plt. 70.

PRESSED OCTAGON (Figure 234)

Maker: Unknown **Y.O.P.:** circa 1890 **Colors made:** crystal and amber **Items made:** further research pending **Repro's:** none **Name by:** *Author*.

PRETTY PANELS (Figure 235)

Maker: Probably Hobbs, Brockunier & Co., (see ad reprint pg. 66) **Y.O.P.:** circa 1890 **Colors made:** crystal, blue and amber — apple green & canary would be rare **Items made:** Only the syrup is shown in the catalogue **Repro's:** none **Name by:** *Author* — further research pending.

PRIMA DONNA (Figure 236)

Maker: Hobbs, Brockunier **Y.O.P.:** circa 1885 **Colors made:** cased vasa murrhine with splashes of cranberry against a white casing **Items made:** to date I have seen the syrup, sugar shaker, cracker jar and toothpick (in the *Ring-Neck* mold)—Peterson shows the salt shaker **Repro's:** none **Name by:** Author **NOTES:** Although more like art glass than pattern glass, I felt this unique line deserved a name by which it could be known. The molds for *Hobbs' Optic* were used in making *Prima Donna*, and the cracker jar is indescribably beautiful (has a domed glass top).

PRISCILLA, FOSTORIA'S (Figure 237)

Maker: Fostoria Glass Co., Moundsville, W. Va. **Y.O.P.:** circa 1900 **Colors made:** crystal and emerald green, often with gold **Items made:** table set, water set, berry set, syrup, toothpick, salt shaker (2 shapes), vase, covered compote, lamps, others **Repro's:** none **Name by:** Orig. Mfr. Name (*Kamm 8*, pg. 200) **NOTE:** The syrup shown here is quite scarce, and not even shown in the recent catalogue reprint of Fostoria's 1901 products.

238
QUILTED PHLOX
(green cased)

239
QUILTED PHLOX
(green cased)

240
QUILTED PHLOX
(amethyst)

241
QUILTED PHLOX
(apple green)

242
QUILTED PHLOX
(decorated milk)

243
REVERSE SWIRL
(blue opales.)

244
REVERSE SWIRL
(cranberry satin)

245
REVERSE SWIRL
(pale blue opaque)

246
REVERSE SWIRL
(deep blue opaque)

247
**REVERSE SWIRL,
COLLARED**
(blue opalescent)

QUILTED PHLOX (Figures 238-242) (See also Figure 362)
Maker: My previous conclusion that this was "Kopp influenced" appears less likely, due to the discovery that *Panelled Sprig* was made by Northwood at Indiana, Pa.—both patterns seem to have common origins. **Y.O.P.:** circa 1894 to 1905 **Colors made:** crystal, amethyst, sapphire blue, apple green and opaque & cased colors of white, green, blue, pink, mauve, yellow (rare), and other experimental possibilities **Items made:** toothpick, salt shaker, sugar shaker, syrup jug (scarce), and a miniature lamp, rose bowl (shaped like the syrup shown here) **Repro's:** none **Name by:** *Warman.*

REVERSE SWIRL (Figures 243-247)
Maker: Both Buckeye Glass Co. and Model Flint Co. (see Book 2) **Y.O.P.:** from 1890 to circa 1900 **Colors made:** white, blue, cranberry,

canary and possibly amber opalescent—sometimes with a beautiful satin finish—also in opaque colors (light & deep blue shown here) **Items made:** see the listing in Book 2—add to that a celery vase and a miniature night lamp **Repro's:** none **Name by:** *BOUL*, plt. 90 **IMPORTANT NOTE:** The possibility exists that *Reverse Swirl* was made by Buckeye in the shape shown on Figure 243, whereas the "collared" version was made by Model Flint Glass. The collared variant can be found in a water pitcher, syrup, sugar shaker & toothpick (Boultinghouse calls it *Ribbon Swirl*), whereas the regular pattern was made in a complete table service. It is odd, however, that the molds for the tall syrup in the *Windows* pattern is identical to the mold on Figure 243 above. The blown opalescent patterns have been, are now, and will continue to be a major source of mystery and doubt in the mind of this researcher.

37

248
REVERSE SWIRL
(speckled, canary)

249
TORPEDO
(ruby-stain)

250
RIBBED OPAL LATTICE
(blue)

251
RIBBED OPAL LATTICE
(cranberry, short)

252
RIB, SCROLLED
(blue opaque)

253
RIBBED PILLAR
(spatter)

254
RIBBED PILLAR
(spatter)

255
RIBBED PILLAR
(blue spatter)

256
RIDGE SWIRL
(amber)

257
RIDGE SWIRL
(cobalt)

REVERSE SWIRL, SPECKLED (Fig. 248)
Makers: The process for this speckled finish was patented by Northwood in November, 1888—while he was associated with Buckeye Glass Co. Shards have been unearthed also at his Indiana, Pa. plant site. Reportedly the pattern was also made at the Albany, Ind. site of the Model Flint Glass Co. (see *BOND*, pg. 4), although production was most definitely limited **Y.O.P.:** from 1888 to circa 1900 **Colors made:** white, blue, canary & cranberry speckled **Items made:** the same as the opalescent version of this pattern, although in considerably more limited quantities **Repro's:** none **Name by:** *Author*.

TORPEDO (Fig. 249)
Maker: Thompson Glass Co., Uniontown, Pa. **Y.O.P.:** circa 1889 **Colors made:** crystal & ruby-stained **Items made:** complete table set, excluding a toothpick holder **Repro's:** none **Name by:** *Kamm 2*, pg. 107 **Other name:** *Pigmy* **NOTES:** It is rather amusing that this syrup, seen in several collections I have studied to date, always has a replaced or reproduction lid on top. The original one must have been made of poor quality metal to have deteriorated so.

RIBBED OPAL LATTICE (Figures 250-251)
Maker: Probably Hobbs or Buckeye, but it's almost impossible to prove on this one **Y.O.P.:** circa 1889 **Colors made:** white, blue & cranberry opalescent **Items made:** see listing Book 2—I failed to note that there are two different sugar shakers, a tall and a short

(Figure 393 & 251) **Repro's:** None **Name by:** *Boultinghouse*, plate 195 **Other name:** *Expanded Diamond*.

RIB SCROLLED (Figure 252)
Maker: Gillinder & Sons **Y.O.P.:** circa 1900 **Colors made:** white, green, & turquoise opaque advertised (see page 86)—any other color would be rare **Items made:** Only sugar shaker & salt shaker known **Repro's:** None **Name by:** *Warman's*.

RIBBED PILLAR (Figure 253-255)
Maker: Either Hobbs or Northwood—the finial on the butter & sugar lid matches the *Royal Ivy* finial **Y.O.P.:** from 1890 **Colors made:** crystal with pink & white spatter (sometimes frosted), and sapphire blue with white spatter **Items made:** table set, water set, berry set, toothpick, sugar shaker, syrup, celery vase, salt shaker **Repro's:** none **Name by:** *Author* **Other name:** *Spatter Glass Pleat* (PET SAL) **NOTE:** The salt shaker & toothpick were advertised in an 1890 Butler Brothers catalogue, and called "Pompeiian," selling for 79¢ a dozen.

RIDGE SWIRL (Figures 256-257) (See also Figure 394)
Maker: Unknown **Y.O.P.:** circa 1900 **Colors made:** crystal, amber, emerald green (see Figure 394), and scarce in cobalt blue **Items made:** only sugar shaker documented to date—further research pending **Repro's:** none **Name by:** *Taylor* (plate 1).

258
RING BAND
(custard)

259
RING NECK
(spatter)

260
RING NECK
(pale spatter)

261
RING NECK
(spatter-IVT)

262
RING NECK
(optic)

263
RING NECK
(stripe, opales.)

264
RING-WAIST
(decorated emerald)

265
ROBIN'S NEST
(amber)

266
ROSE PETALS
(pink cased)

267
ROSE PETALS
(pink satin)

RING BAND (Figure 258)
Maker: A. H. Heisey Glass Co. **Y.O.P.:** circa 1900 **Colors made:** this pattern is only found in custard glass, but with several variations in decoration **Items made:** water set, table set, berry set, cruet set (cruet, salt & pepper on tray), celery vase (rare), jelly compote, assorted souvenir items **Repro's:** none **Name by:** *PET SAL*, pg. 170-J.

RING NECK SPATTER (Figure 259-261)
Maker: Hobbs, Brockunier & Co. **Y.O.P.:** circa 1890 **Colors made:** the *Ring Neck* mold was used on several pieces of other Hobbs' patterns (the *Optic* and *Prima Donna* toothpicks—see Book 1), but the spatter version is a crystal background with splashes of cranberry & white swirling through. The color can be very deep (Fig. 259) or very pale (Fig. 260) **Items made:** complete table setting **Repro's:** none **Name by:** *PET SAL*, pg. 170-K **NOTES:** Figure 261 is unusually different, as it has distinct inverted thumbprints inside, which may not show up well in the photograph.

RING NECK OPTIC (Figure 262)
Maker: Probably Hobbs **Y.O.P.:** circa 1890 **Colors made:** green, blue and cranberry **Items made:** not ascertainable at this time **Repro's:** none **Name by:** *Author*.

RING NECK STRIPE (Figure 263)
See Figures 288-293 for data concerning this pattern.

RING-WAIST BASE (Figure 264)
Maker: Uncertain **Y.O.P.:** circa 1895 **Colors made:** emerald green, amber and blue, usually enamel-decorated **Items made:** the syrup shown here and a miniature lamp *(SM MIN,* pg. 189) only items documented to date—a sugar shaker is likely **Repro's:** none **Name by:** *Author*.

ROBIN'S NEST (Figure 265)
Maker: Unknown **Y.O.P.:** circa 1890 **Colors made:** blue, apple green, crystal, amber, & canary **Items made:** the syrup is the only item documented to date **Repro's:** none **Name by:** *Author*.

ROSE PETALS (Figure 266-267)
Maker: Fostoria Lamp & Shade Co., Fostoria, Ohio (later to become the Consolidated Lamp & Glass Co.) **Y.O.P.:** the design for this pattern was patented in March, 1891 by Nicholas Kopp, Jr. **Colors made:** the *Pink Rose* was made primarily in the color from which its named is derived, satin, cased and opaque pink—any other color would be extremely rare if it exists **Items made:** sugar shaker & salt shaker **Repro's:** none **Name by:** *Author, (PET SAL,* pg. 58 calls this "Pink Rose".)

268
ROYAL IVY
(frosted rubina)

269
ROYAL IVY
(frosted rubina)

270
ROYAL IVY
(cased spatter)

271
ROYAL IVY
(cased spatter)

272
ROYAL IVY
(rainbow cracquelle)

273
ROYAL OAK
(frosted rubina)

274
ROYAL OAK
(frosted rubina)

275
SAWTOOTH HONEYCOMB
(ruby-stain)

276
SCROLL & NET
(WITH COSMOS)
(pidgeon blood)

277
SCROLL & NET
(decorated milk)

ROYAL IVY (Figures 268-272)
Maker: Northwood   **Y.O.P.:** originally at his Martins Ferry location, circa 1889 — the cracquelle version was made at the Ellwood, Pa. location, circa 1894   **Colors made:** frosted crystal, plain rubina, rubina frosted, rainbow cased, rainbow cracquelle, frosted rainbow cracquelle, very rare in frosted with amber-stained ivy (see page   ), and in clambroth opaline   **Items made:** table set, water set, berry set, syrup, sugar shaker, toothpick, salt shaker, cruet, night lamp, pickle caster, jam jar   **Repro's:** none   **Name by:** *Kamm 5*, pg. 87   **NOTE:** the insert to the pickle caster is the same piece used as the spooner to the table set.

ROYAL OAK (Figures 273-274)
Maker: Northwood   **Y.O.P.:** circa 1889   **Colors made:** frosted crystal, glossy rubina and satin rubina   **Items made:** table set, water set, berry set, toothpick, salt shaker, cruet, syrup, pickle caster   **Repro's:** none   **Name by:** Orig. Mfr. name, (see *Kamm 5*, plate 20)   **NOTE:** see Book 1 for notes concerning the confusion over the so-called "Jewel" line—reportedly a variant of *Royal Oak* without acorns in the pattern.

SAWTOOTHED HONEYCOMB (Figure 275)
Maker: Steiner Glass Co., Buckhannon, W. Va. and reportedly later by the Union Stopper Co., at Morgantown   **Y.O.P.:** circa 1906 to 1908   **Colors made:** crystal and ruby-stained   **Items made:** indeter-

minate at this time — no celery or cruet known   **Repro's:** none   **Name by:** *Kamm 1*, pg. 115.

SCROLL & NET (Figure 276-277)
Maker: Research pending   **Y.O.P.:** circa 1900   **Colors made:** decorated milk glass, opaque colors, and rare in pigeon blood red   **Items made:** salt shaker, syrup jug   **Repro's:** Peterson says the salt shaker has been reproduced, but I have no further information to offer here   **Name by:** *Warmans*   **NOTE:** With the blown out flowers on the pattern, it should be referred to as "Scroll & Net with Cosmos."

SEAWEED, OPALESCENT (Figures 278-279)
Makers: Known production by Beaumont, probably from reissued Hobb's molds (note the *Bulbous Base* mold—see page 52)—production also undergone at Northwood Glass, while at Wheeling   **Y.O.P.:** circa 1895 to 1905   **Colors made:** white, blue & cranberry opales., rarely with a satin finish   **Items made:** see listing in Book 2—I failed to note the barber & bitters bottles and the miniature lamp   **Repro's:** none   **Name by:** *Taylor*, plate 12   **Other name:** *Beaumont's Beauty.*

SCROLL WITH CANE BAND (Figure 280)
Maker: West Virginia Glass Co.   **Y.O.P.:** circa 1895 to 1900   **Colors made:** crystal, two shades of ruby-staining, amber-stained and rare in emerald green   **Items made:** complete table service, including open & covered high-standard compotes, cruet, toothpick, etc.   **Repro's:** none   **Name by:** *Kamm 3*, pg. 92.

(continued next page)

278
SEAWEED, OPALES.
(cranberry)

279
SEAWEED, OPALES.
(blue)

280
SCROLL WITH CANE BAND
(amber-stain)

281
SIX-PANEL FINECUT
(amber-stain)

282
SKIRTED PYRAMID
(emerald)

283
SPANISH LACE
(blue—old reeded handle)

284
SPANISH LACE
(wide-waist, cranberry)

285
SYNORA LACE
(red satin)

286
SYNORA LACE
(decorated milk)

287
S-REPEAT
(apple green)

(continued from previous page)

SIX-PANEL FINE-CUT (Figure 281)
Maker: Dalzell, Gilmore & Leighton **Y.O.P.:** circa 1890 (advertised by Butler Brothers that year) **Colors made:** clear & amber-stained **Items made:** a considerable variety, although I have never seen a salt shaker, toothpick or cruet—very few patterns made at Findlay had toothpicks as part of the set **Repro's:** none **Name by:** *SM FIN*, pg. 72.

SKIRTED PYRAMID (Figure 282)
Maker: Unknown **Y.O.P.:** circa 1895 **Colors made:** speculative—emerald green (illus.), amber, blue **Items made:** only sugar shaker shown documented to date **Repro's:** none **Name by:** *Author*—I hesitated calling it this, because other matching items may be shaped completely different.

SPANISH LACE (Figures 283-284)
Maker: After considerable research, and a bit of luck, I can now offer some documentable evidence. This pattern was originally made in England, in the famous Stourbridge area, and the pattern was copied here by Northwood. I feel he first introduced it during his tenure at Buckeye, and re-issued it later at his Indiana, Pa. factory shards have been found there in this pattern) and again later at Wheeling, W. Va. **Y.O.P.:** from 1885 to as late as 1920 **Colors made:** white, blue, canary & cranberry opalescent—rare in green opalescent (the English pieces—primarily vases—were mostly in vaseline, and had heavy opalescence) **Items made:** see listing Book 2—a rose bowl and

a miniature lamp were also made, as well as the English vases of all sizes **Repro's:** none, unless you consider the late Northwood (after 1920) a reproduction. At any rate, there is no *new Spanish Lace* on the market. **Name by:** Popular Nomenclature (may be the original name, passed down through the years) **Other name:** *Queen's Lace (Taylor)*.

SYNORA LACE (Figures 285-286)
Maker: Ohio Flint Glass Works, Lancaster, Ohio (while operated by National Glass) **Y.O.P.:** circa 1901 **Colors made:** decorated milk glass and rare in red satin **Items made:** salt shaker & syrup jug known **Repro's:** none **Name by:** *Author* **NOTE:** See ad reprint on page 85.

S-REPEAT (Figure 287)
Maker: Northwood Company, at Indiana, Pa. (while operated by National Glass Co.) **Y.O.P.:** circa 1900 to as late as 1910 **Colors made:** crystal, light & dark amethyst, apple & yellow-green, pale & sapphire blue—these variations in color the result of such extended production **Items made:** see listing Book 2, pg. 23 **Repro's:** new cruets & toothpicks on the market, with the toothpick capable of fooling even the most astute collector (in certain colors) **Name by:** *Kamm 4*, pg. 115 **NOTE:** Production of this pattern was undoubtedly continued after Northwood quit National Glass. The factory later was called the Dugan Glass Works, and the new owners undoubtedly retained many original Northwood molds and continued their production. This also explains the difference in colors.

288
STRIPE, BULBOUS
(vaseline)

289
STRIPE, RING NECK
(cranberry)
(old!)

290
STRIPE (REPRO)
(blue)

291
STRIPE, TALL
(blue)

292
STRIPE, OPALES.
(blue)

293
STRIPE, OPALES.
(vaseline)

294
STRIPE, WIDE
(green)

295
STRIPE, WIDE
(blue)

296
STRIPE, WIDE
(cranberry)

297
SUNK HONEYCOMB
(ruby-stain)

STRIPE, OPALESCENT (Figures 288-293)
Maker: Primary production by Hobbs—possible additional production by Buckeye & Northwood **Y.O.P.:** from circa 1888 to 1900 **Colors made:** white, blue, canary & cranberry opalescent—would be rare in green or rubina **Items made:** water set, syrup (3 shapes), toothpick (see Book 1), barber bottle, salt shakers, caster bottle set, celery vase with ruffled top, and a sugar shaker (the last two not listed in Book 2) **Repro's:** see Figure 290—new syrups in cranberry & blue have a double bulbous ring neck and the thin stripes tend to separate. Also note the difference in the handles. Believe these are imported by A & A, but not absolutely sure. **Name by:** *Author* **Other names:** *Candy Stripe, Ribbon Stripe.*

STRIPE, WIDE (Figures 294-296)
Maker: Primarily by Hobbs, but so many of their patterns were re-issued later it is difficult to tell who else may have made this pattern **Y.O.P.:** circa 1888 to 1900 **Colors made:** white, blue, cranberry & green opalescent—canary has not been documented **Items made:** water set, syrup (2 shapes), sugar shaker, cruet, toothpick holder (see Book 1), and possibly others **Repro's:** none to date **Name by:** *Taylor*, plate 1 **NOTE:** This pattern can also be found with Hobb's *Venetian Diamond* pattern in the glass (see Book 2—395). A syrup or sugar shaker in this variant would be rare.

SUNK HONEYCOMB (Figure 297)
Maker: Originally by Greensburg Glass, Greensburg, Pa.—also by McKee at Jeannette, Pa. **Y.O.P.:** circa 1900 **Colors made:** crystal and ruby-stained, rare amber-stained, sometimes etched **Items made:** table set, water set, berry set, cruet, toothpick, individual cream & sugar, syrup, goblet, wine, salt shaker **Repro's:** none **Name by:** *Kamm 2*, pg. 57 **Original name:** Corona **Note:** an ad reprinted in *Kamm 6*, plate 45 reveals this to have been originally a Greensburg pattern. Molds were undoubtedly transferred during the National Glass Co. association.

298	299	300	301	302
SUNSET (blue opaque)	**SWASTIKA** (green opalescent)	**SWIRL, CAMPHOR**	**SWIRL, OPALES.** (cranberry)	**SWIRL, OPALES.** (cranberry)

303	304	305	306	307
SWIRL, OPALES. (bulbous base)	**SWIRL, OPALES.** (bulbous base)	**SWIRL, OPALES.** (Northwood)	**SWIRL, OPALES.** (tapered)	**SWIRL & LEAF** (white opaque)

SUNSET (Figure 298) (See also Figure 398)
Maker: Dithridge **Y.O.P.:** beginning in 1894 **Colors made:** opaque white, blue, pink and custard (see Figure 398) — also cased glass colors **Items made:** syrup pitcher, salt shaker, toothpick holder, lamp **Repro's:** none **Name by:** *PET SAL*, pg. 40-U **NOTE:** The custard in this pattern is quite rare.

SWASTIKA (Figure 299)
Maker: Either Buckeye or Northwood **Y.O.P.:** circa 1890 to 1900 **Colors made:** white, cranberry & green opalescent — haven't seen blue yet **Items made:** water set, syrup pitcher — all very rare **Repro's:** none **Name by:** Taylor, plate 13.

SWIRL, CAMPHOR (Figure 300)
Maker: Hobbs **Y.O.P.:** circa 1888 **Colors made:** this is the *Frances Ware Swirl* mold without any amber-staining **Items made:** same as *Frances Ware Swirl* **Repro's:** none **Name by:** *Kamm 6*, pg. 68 (*Blown Swirl*).

SWIRL, OPALESCENT (Figures 301-306)
Makers: Originally by Hobbs — reissued molds by Beaumont; additional production by Jefferson Glass after 1900, and shards have been found in this line at Northwood's Indiana, Pa. site **Y.O.P.:** from 1888 to 1910 **Colors made:** white, blue, canary, rubina, cranberry & green opalescent **Items made:** see listing in Book 2 — note that there are 4 different shaped sugar shakers and there are 3 different shaped water pitchers **Repro's:** several by L. G. Wright & Fenton **Name by:** Popular nomenclature.

SWIRL & LEAF (Figure 307)
Maker: Incorrectly attributed in Book 1 — this pattern must have been made by the same company which made *Quilted Phlox*, and I no longer believe that to be late Hobbs (Kopp). An educated guess would be Northwood, although he was not known for too much of this type ware **Y.O.P.:** circa 1890 to 1900 **Colors made:** white, blue, green, pink, and a rare yellow and grey opaque — also made in cased glass colors, which match exactly *Quilted Phlox* colors **Items made:** the above syrup is a rare unlisted item — also made in a salt shaker and toothpick holder **Repro's:** none **Name by:** *PET SAL*, pg. 40-W.

308
THOUSAND DIAMONDS
(apple green)

309
1000 EYE
(amber)

310
THREADED RUBINA
(Northwood)

311
TORQUAY
(pidgeon blood satin)

312
TOPPLING PILLARS
(spatter)

313
TUBBY OPTIC
(green)

314
TUBBY OPTIC
(blue)

315
UTOPIA OPTIC
(green)

316
UTOPIA OPTIC
(green)

317
VALENCIA WAFFLE
(apple green)

THOUSAND DIAMONDS (Figure 308)
Maker: Not previously listed—this is George Duncan & Sons #317 pattern, with production continued by U.S. Glass Co. **Y.O.P.:** circa 1890 **Colors made:** crystal, blue & apple green **Items made:** the syrup shown here and the water set are the only items I am able to document at this time — no other items appear in the catalogue **Repro's:** none **Name by:** *Author* **NOTE:** It's a real thrill to introduce a new pattern, and this one certainly is unusual with the raised diamond quilting. See ad reprint page 78.

THOUSAND EYE (Figure 309)
Maker: Probably Adams & Co., with production continued after U.S. Glass takeover **Y.O.P.:** circa 1880 to 1895 **Colors made:** crystal, canary, apple green, blue & amber **Items made:** too many to mention here **Repro's:** some—but not the syrup **Name by:** Popular Nomenclature — *LEE EAPG* **NOTE:** There are several variants of this pattern, with only minute differences to tell them apart. See the cruets on page 57.

THREADED RUBINA SWIRL (Figure 310)
Maker: This researcher feels it is Northwood—the Oglebay Institute says it is Hobbs **Y.O.P.:** circa 1890 **Colors made:** only rubina known (cranberry at top, clear at bottom) **Items made:** Water set, table set, berry set, toothpick, sugar shaker, syrup, salt shaker, cruet (rare), celery vase **Repro's:** none **Name by:** *Author* (earlier I called this *Threaded Rubina*) **IMPORTANT ATTRIBUTION NOTE:** Except for the syrup shown here, every piece made in this pattern is identical in shape to corresponding pieces of Leaf Umbrella.

TORQUAY (Figure 311)
Maker: Strong possibility that this is Consolidated Lamp & Glass (definitely Kopp) **Y.O.P.:** circa 1904 **Colors made:** pigeon blood red, pigeon blood satin, cobalt blue decorated, white satin decorated **Items made:** table set, berry set, cracker jar, syrup jug, salt shaker, cruet, water pitcher, tumblers, celery vase (most pieces have metal tops & bases) **Repro's:** none **Name by:** *Author* **NOTE:** The original spring lid on this syrup is patent dated exactly like others which were used by Kopp.

TOPPLING PILLARS (Figure 312)
Maker: Probably Hobbs **Y.O.P.:** circa 1890 **Colors made:** only spatter (pink & white on crystal) known **Items made:** further research pending **Repro's:** none **Name by:** *Author* **NOTE:** The distinctive blue reeded handle (an old one, believe me), and the typical Hobbs spring lid.

TUBBY OPTIC (Figures 313-314)
Maker: Beaumont Glass Co. **Y.O.P.:** circa 1895 **Colors made:** cranberry, blue and emerald green decorated **Items made:** syrup only **Name by:** *Author* **NOTE:** see the Beaumont catalogue reprint on page 61.

UTOPIA OPTIC (Figures 315-316)
Maker: Either Buckeye or Northwood **Y.O.P.:** circa 1892 **Colors made:** green, blue and possibly cranberry, all decorated **Items made:** syrup, sugar shaker & miniature night lamp **Repro's:** none **Name by:** *Author* **NOTE:** The old reeded handle on the syrup, identical in shape to *Spanish Lace*. Also, the sugar shaker is in the "Wide-Waist" mold, also typical of all *Spanish Lace* sugar shakers.

(continued on next page)

318 **VENECIA** (cranberry)	**319** **VENECIA** (green to clear)	**320** **VENETIAN DIAMOND** (cranberry)	**321** **VENETIAN DIAMOND** (ring neck)	**322** **VENETIAN DIAMOND** (spatter)
323 **VICTORIA, RIVERSIDE** (ruby-stained)	**324** **VINING ROSE** (muranese)	**325** **WEDDING BELLS** (rose-flashed)	**326** **WEST VIRGINIA OPTIC** (amethyst)	**327** **WEST VIRGINIA OPTIC** (green)

(continued from previous page)

VALENCIA WAFFLE (Figure 317)
Maker: Adams & Company's #85 pattern, reissued in 1891 by U.S. Glass **Y.O.P.:** circa 1885 to 1895 **Colors made:** crystal, amber, blue, apple green & canary **Items made:** A considerable service — with no toothpick or cruet known **Repro's:** None **Name by:** *Millard* **Other name:** Kamm calls this *Block & Star* **NOTE:** see catalogue reprint on page 83 which was responsible for attribution of this pattern. *LEE* calls this *Hexagonal Block.*

VENECIA (Figures 318-319)
Maker: Uncertain at this time **Y.O.P.:** circa 1890 **Items made:** salt shaker, sugar shaker, cruet, & toothpick holder are the only items I have seen to date **Colors made:** rubina (cranberry to clear), cranberry and green to clear documented to date **Repro's:** none **Name by:** *Author* **NOTE:** This is not really pattern glass, but the matching items in such beautiful colors make it worthy of carrying a name all its own. Also noteworthy is that the lids on these examples shown here are frequently found on Northwood sugar shakers, although this can hardly be considered conclusive.

VENETIAN DIAMOND (Figures 320-322)
Maker: Hobbs, Brockunier & Co. **Y.O.P.:** circa 1887 **Colors made:** primarily in cranberry, also found in Hobbs pink & white spatter **Items made:** Syrup, sugar shaker, cruet, certainly others **Repro's:** possibly — I have seen a questionable sugar shaker in the *Nine-Panel* mold in *Venetian Diamond* **Name by:** popular nomenclature **Other name:** *Diamond Quilt* (this name should be withheld for the pressed version of this pattern) **NOTE:** Notice the Hobbs syrup top again here.

VICTORIA, RIVERSIDE'S (Figure 323)
Maker: Riverside Glass Co. **Y.O.P.:** circa 1898 **Colors made:** crystal, ruby-stained & amber-stained **Items made:** water set, table set, berry set, high-standard compote (open or covered), cruet, toothpick, salt shaker, jelly compote, celery, goblet **Repro's:** none **Other name:** *Draped Top* or *Draped Red Top* **NOTE:** This pattern is one of the "elite" among collector's of ruby-stained glass.

VINING ROSE (Figure 324)
Maker: New Martinsville Glass Co. **Y.O.P.:** circa 1898 **Colors made:** "salmon" muranese (a type of art glass), blue opaque, probably other opaque colors **Items made:** syrup & salt shakers **Repro's:** none **Name by:** *Miller,* Fig. 9 & 22 **NOTE:** This one is really rare!

WEDDING BELLS (Figure 325)
Maker: Fostoria Glass Co. **Y.O.P.:** circa 1900 **Colors made:** crystal, cranberry-flashed **Items made:** complete table service, including a punch bowl & cups **Repro's:** none **Name by:** Orig. Mfr. Name.

WEST VIRGINIA'S OPTIC (Figures 326-327)
Maker: West Virginia Glass Co. **Y.O.P.:** circa 1895 **Colors made:** emerald green, crystal, amethyst & rare in cobalt blue & cranberry **Items made:** complete table set — although some pieces had limited production **Repro's:** none **Name by:** *Kamm 6,* pg. 49 **NOTE:** This "Optic" mold was used on a variant of *Daisy & Fern* and *Blown Twist.*

328
WIDE-WAIST
(amethyst)

329
WILD IRIS
(decorated milk)

330
WILD ROSE, Fostoria
(decorated milk)

331
WILDFLOWER
(blue)

332
WINTER MORNING GLORY
(decorated milk)

333
WINDOWS, SWIRLED
(cranberry, short)

334
WINDOWS, SWIRLED
(cranberry)

335
WINGED SCROLL
(custard)

336
X-RAY
(emerald)

337
ZIPPER BORDERS
(ruby-stained)

WIDE WAIST (Figure 328)
Maker: Either Buckeye or Northwood **Y.O.P.:** circa 1890 to 1900
Colors made: blue, amethyst, and possible cranberry **Items made:**
the name applies only to the sugar shaker, which has a wide-waisted
shape **Repro's:** none **Name by:** *Author* **NOTE:** This mold was
also used for *Spanish Lace, Daisy & Fern, Blown Twist.*

WILD IRIS (Figure 329)
Maker: Uncertain—further research pending **Y.O.P.:** circa 1902
Colors made: decorated milk glass in several color variations **Items
made:** Water set, table set, berry set, syrup, salt shaker, cracker jar,
others **Repro's:** None **Name by:** *Warman.*

WILD ROSE, FOSTORIA'S (Figure 330)
Maker: Fostoria Glass Co. **Y.O.P.:** circa 1900-1905 **Colors made:**
decorated milk glass—would be rare if made in red satin **Items
made:** syrup, salt shaker, toothpick **Repro's:** none **Name by:** *Author.*

WILDFLOWER (Figure 331)
Maker: Adams & Company, with production continued by U.S. Glass
Y.O.P.: circa 1885 to 1900 **Colors made:** crystal, amber, blue, apple
green, canary **Items made:** complete table set, except for a cruet
& toothpick holder **Repro's:** several through the years—some
items being made which were never even made originally (the tiny
oblong salt dip) **Name by:** *LEE VG*, plate 6 **NOTE:** See the amber
syrup in Figure 399. The syrup has never been reproduced.

WINTER MORNING GLORY (Figure 332)
Maker: Fostoria's #176 syrup **Y.O.P.:** circa 1900 **Colors made:**

decorated milk glass **Items made:** only syrup shown here documented to date **Repro's:** none **Name by:** *Author.*

WINDOWS, OPALESCENT (Figure 333-334)
Maker: Originally by Hobbs, although it is impossible to rule out later
production by another firm (Beaumont made a variant without the
swirls) **Y.O.P.:** circa 1888 to 1895 **Colors made:** white, blue and
cranberry opalescent **Items made:** See listing in Book 2 **Repro's:**
The variant without the swirls is being reproduced by L. G. Wright—
beware of the bulbous syrup with the reeded handle—I have never
seen one which I was convinced could be old **Name by:** *Boultinghouse,* plate 190 **NOTE:** Sometimes the little "dots" can be quite
large—but more often they are very tiny.

WINGED SCROLL (Figure 335)
Maker: A. J. Heisey Glass Co. **Y.O.P.:** circa 1888 to 1905 **Colors
made:** crystal (scarce), emerald green, custard and very rare in milk
glass (opal), vaseline **Items made:** every shape imaginable—including a smokers set, a celery vase, cake stand **Repro's:** don't dare fall
for those ridiculous miniature butter dishes in crown tuscan and other
colors—courtesy of Guernsey Glass Co. (for another firm) **Name by:**
Popular Nomenclature **Other name:** *Ivorina Verde* (applicable only
to the custard color).

X-RAY (Figure 336)
Maker: Riverside Glass Co. **Y.O.P.:** circa 1899 to 1902 **Colors made:**
crystal, emerald green and scarce in amethyst—all usually with gold
Items made: Table set, water set (tumblers or goblets), berry set,
cruet, toothpick, syrup (previously unlisted & very rare), salt shaker,
high-standard compote, jelly compote, cruet set on clover-leaf tray,

(continued next page)

New England Glass Examples

338
BULBOUS SATINA

339
COCKLESHELL

340
EGG, MT. WASHINGTON

341
EGG—BASED
(Belleware)

342
EGG—BASED
(Belleware)

343
FIG

344
GILLINDER MELON

345
SMITH BROTHER'S MELON

346
TOMATO

347
OSTRICH EGG

(continued from previous page)

breakfast creamer & covered sugar, celery vase **Repro's:** none **Name by:** Orig. Mfr. name.

ZIPPER BORDERS (Figure 337)
Maker: Uncertain, although I strongly suspect U.S. Glass because of the fern etching (Millard is frequently fern-etched) **Y.O.P.:** circa 1898 **Colors made:** crystal & ruby-stained **Items made:** syrup only item I can validate at this time **Repro's:** none **Name by:** *Author*.

BULBOUS SATINA (Figure 338)
Maker: Uncertain **Y.O.P.:** circa 1890 **Name by:** *Author*.

COCKLESHELL (Figure 339)
Maker: Mt. Washington Glass Co. **Y.O.P.:** circa 1890 **Colors made:** decorated opal—quite rare in satin crystal, cranberry, vaseline, blue and possibly green **Items made:** salt shakers, sugar shakers **Repro's:** none **Name by:** *Pet Sal*, pg. 39-J **NOTE:** The salt shakers had a little metal frame on which to mount the pair. It is not known if the sugar shaker shown had a frame to hold it upright, and thus prevent spillage of sugar through the top. This sugar shaker is extremely rare in any color.

EGG, MT. WASHINGTON (Figure 340)
Maker: Mt. Washington Glass Co. **Y.O.P.:** circa 1890 **Colors made:** primarily in satin and shiny "eggshell" white—scarce examples in colored glass, usually satin finished **Items made:** salt shaker and sugar shaker **Repro's:** none **Name by:** Popular Nomenclature.

EGG-BASED (Figures 341-342)
Maker: Probably Belleware **Y.O.P.:** circa 1895 **Colors made:** only

decorated opalware known **Items:** sugar shaker, syrup, tall salt shakers **Repro's:** none **Name by:** *Author*.

FIG (Figure 343)
Maker: Mt. Washington Glass Co. **Y.O.P.:** circa 1893 **Colors made:** the same colors as the *Cockleshell* **Items made:** salt shaker, sugar shaker, toothpick **Repro's:** none **Name by:** *Pet Sal*, pg. 160-R.

GILLINDER'S MELON (Figure 344)
Maker: Gillinder & Sons **Y.O.P.:** circa 1895 **Colors made:** only decorated opal **Items made:** sugar shakers, salt shakers **Repro's:** None **Name by:** *Author*.

SMITH BROTHER'S MELON (Figure 345)
Maker: Smith Brothers **Y.O.P.:** circa 1895 **Colors made:** only in a pale beige satiny opal **Items made:** sugar shaker, syrup, salt shaker, salt dip, cracker jar, possibly others **Repro's:** none **Name by:** *Author* **Note:** This line is frequently found with the rampant lion trademark of this company.

TOMATO (Figure 346)
Maker: Mt. Washington Glass Co. **Y.O.P.:** patented in December, 1890 **Colors made:** decorated opalware **Items made:** salt shakers, sugar shakers (the patent called it a "sugar box") **Repro's:** none **Name by:** *Pet Sal*, pg. 42-J.

OSTRICH EGG (Figure 347)
Maker: Undoubtedly Mt. Washington, very much like their Royal Flemish **Y.O.P.:** circa 1893 **Colors made:** not certain—this egg is smaller than the figure 340 egg **Repro's:** none **Name by:** *Author*.

348	349	350	351	352
ALBA (blue)	**CHICK-IN-EGG** (decorated)	**GUTTATE** (green satin)	**JEWELLED MOON & STAR** (color-stained)	**LEAFY BASE** (decorated milk)

353	354	355	356	357
LITTLE SHRIMP (white satin)	**QUILTED PHLOX** (pink-cased)	**REVERSE SWIRL** (vaseline opales.)	**SWIRL, OPALES.** (blue tapered)	**TWO-PLY SWIRL** (rose-flashed)

ALBA (Figure 348)
See pattern notes on page 14.

CHICK-IN-EGG (Figure 349)
Maker: Mt. Washington Glass Co. **Y.O.P.:** circa 1893 **Colors made:** decorated opalware **Items made:** salt shakers & rare sugar shaker **Repro's:** none **Name by:** *Author* **Note:** the Chick Head salt shaker was also made in full-bodied variation.

GUTTATE (Figure 350)
Maker: Consolidated Lamp & Glass (see pattern notes on page 26) **Notes:** the syrup shown here is in an unusual green opaque satin—not cased.

JEWELLED MOON & STAR (Figure 351)
Maker: Cooperative Flint Glass Co., Beaver Falls, Pa. **Y.O.P.:** circa 1897 **Colors made:** crystal and decorated crystal—sometimes with frosted "moons" **Items made:** complete table service—however, no toothpick is known to have been made in this variant of "Moon & Star" **Name by:** *Metz 2*, pg. 211 **Original name:** Imperial **Other name:** *Moon & Star Variation* (Lee) **Note:** Kamm reports that this pattern was originally made by the Wilson Glass Co. of Tarentum, Pa. circa 1890, and the molds were acquired afterward by Cooperative.

LEAFY BASE (Figure 352)
Maker: Uncertain **Y.O.P.:** circa 1900 **Colors made:** decorated milk

glass **Items made:** not certain—probably only the syrup and a salt shaker **Repro's:** none **Name by:** *Author*.

LITTLE SHRIMP (Figure 353)
Maker: see pattern notes on page 31. This is an unusual art glass-like version of this pattern, similar to Mt. Washington.

QUILTED PHLOX (Figure 354)
See pattern notes on page 37. Shown here is a lovely deep pink cased piece of this pattern.

REVERSE SWIRL (Figure 355)
See pattern notes on page 37. Shown here is the odd shade of canary opalescent which is sometimes confused for amber opalescent. The canary shade often varies from a very pale yellow to a very deep lemon yellow to this muddy yellow.

SWIRL, OPALESCENT (Figure 356)
See pattern notes on page 43. Shown here is the tapered version of the sugar shaker which is identical in shape to Hobbs ware.

TWO-PLY SWIRL (Figure 357)
Maker: Duncan & Miller Glass Co., Washington, Pa. **Y.O.P.:** advertised in 1902 **Colors made:** crystal, crystal with gold, crystal with amethyst-flashed panels **Items made:** a quite large table service **Repro's:** none **Name by:** *Pet Sal*, pg. 41-J.

Milk Glass Syrups
(& sugar shaker)

358 PANELLED SPRIG (H)	**359** ENCIRCLED SCROLL (H)	**360** ELONGATED DROPS (W)	**361** FOSTORIA'S #1008 (H)	**362** PEARLY PANELS & FLOWER (Fostoria #1009) (H)	**363** BANDED SHELLS (H)

364 RIBS OVER RIBS (H)	**365** DITHRIDGE #25 (H)	**366** NETTED RIBBONS (H)	**367** DOUBLE RIB (M)	**368** WEST VIRGINIA'S OPTIC (K)

369 KNOTTY BULB (P)	**370** PRIMROSE & PEARLS (H)	**371** KNOBBY (M)	**372** RINGS & RIBS (H)	**373** FANCY FANS (H)

Names by: (H) Author, (W) Warman, (M) Millard, (K) Kamm, (P) Peterson

text provided on the above.

374
ROSE-IN-RELIEF
(H)
Fostoria

375
LACY FLORAL
(K)
tall

376
FRENCH PRIMROSE
(H)

377
CHAIN & SWAG
(H)

378
GIANT DOGWOOD
(H)

379
SERENDIPITY
(H)

380
STRAWBERRY PATCH
(H)

381
**FRENCH FLEUR-
DE-LIS**
(H)

382
BEADED HEXAGON
(H)

383
HIDING BUTTERFLY
(H)

384
STIPPLED DAHLIA
(P)

385
LACY FLORAL
(K)

386
PETUNIA SWIRL
(H)

387
CATHERINE ANN
(H)

Names by: (H) Author, (W) Warman, (M) Millard, (K) Kamm, (P) Peterson

*No text provided on the above.

388	389	390	391	392	393
ACORN DIAMONDS (amber) U.S. Glass—1891	**FLOWER MOLD** (green)	**INVERTED THUMB-PRINT** (decorated)	**LIBBEY'S MAIZE** (decorated opal)	**QUILTED PHLOX** (pink opaque)	**RIBBED OPAL LATTICE** (tall)

394	395	396	397	398	399
RIDGE SWIRL (green)	**ROPE & RIBS** (amber)	**ROPE & THUMBPRINT** (blue)	**ROPE & THUMBPRINT** (amber)	**SUNSET** (custard)	**WILDFLOWER** (amber)

400	401	402	403	404	405
(satin scenic decorated)	(spatter)	(tortoise shell)	(vaseline decor.)	(blue spatter)	(cranberry decorated)

The Hobb's Coloratura Series

Late Additions

Fig. #405-A
Decorated opaque "COREOPSIS", tall
(see text page 21)

Fig. #405-B
Unfrosted pigeon blood "TORQUAY"
(see text page 44)

(Photo by Jack Hall Photography)

Fig. #405-C
Extremely rare amber-stained
"ROYAL IVY"
(see text page 40)

(Photo courtesy C. Coffey)

Fig. #405-D
Rare Blue Opalescent "POINSETTA"
(see text page 35)

(Photo courtesy D. Carney)

Cruet Addenda

The following small section is merely a listing of cruets which are significant to my research or which were unlisted in the two books devoted to the subject of cruets by Dean L. Murray. Mr. Murray is a personal friend of mine and in no way am I trying to present a competitive publication. In fact, I highly recommend his second book "More Cruets Only" to anyone who follows this series. This follow-up to his first book "Cruets Only" illustrates and identifies literally hundreds and hundreds of cruets, most of them very very rare. The addenda presented here is called just that, as it includes only unlisted cruets, or those which are historically significant to my research reports, thus serving as an addenda to the Murray book.

Anyone who wishes to purchase a copy of Mr. Murray's books on cruets can send me a blank stamped envelope, and I will direct your letter to the proper channels.

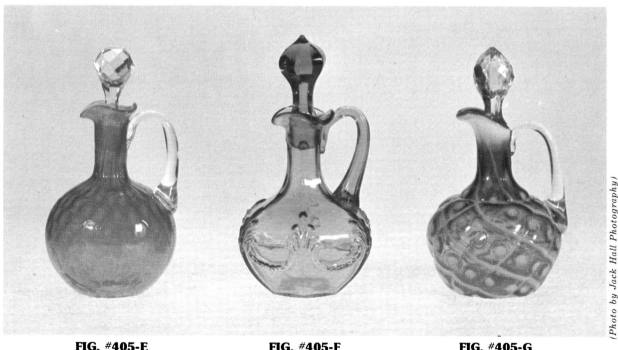

(Photo by Jack Hall Photography)

FIG. #405-E
OPALESCENT DIAMONDS
(Hobbs—1880's)

FIG. #405-F
FOSTORIA'S PRISCILLA
(see text pg. 36)

FIG. #405-G
COINSPOT & SWIRL
(Northwood Mold)

406
**APPLE & GRAPE
IN SCROLL**
(o.s.)

407
**NORTHWOOD'S
BEADED CIRCLED**
(o.s.)

408
**BEADED OVALS
IN SAND**
(o.s.)

409
BEADED SWAG
(o.s.)

410
**BELLAIRE
BASKETWEAVE**
(n.o.s.)

411
**BELMONT
DIAMOND**
(o.s.)

412
**BELMONT'S
REFLECTING FAN**
(o.s.)

413
BEATTY HONEYCOMB
(o.s.)

414
**BLOCK,
FOSTORIA'S**
(o.s.)

415
BLOCK, COOP
(o.s.)

416
BRAZILLIAN
(o.s.)

417
BUTTON PANEL
(o.s.)

418
COLUMN BLOCK
(o.s.)

419
CIRCLED SCROLL
(n.o.s.)

APPLE & GRAPE IN SCROLL (Figure 406)
Maker: Probably Fostoria Glass **Y.O.P.:** circa 1905 **Colors made:** crystal and green known **Items made:** further research pending **Repro's:** none **Name by:** Uncertain **Note:** The original stopper is exactly the same as the one found in the *Brazilian* cruet: thus, my attribution.

BEADED CIRCLE, NORTHWOOD'S (Figure 407)
Maker: Northwood **Y.O.P.:** circa 1904 **Colors made:** crystal, apple green, pale blue, rare in amethyst & custard **Items made:** Water set, table set, berry set, cruet, salt shaker, jelly compote **Repro's:** none **Name by:** Popular Nomenclature **Note:** The name of Northwood should always precede the pattern name to avoid confusing this with other similarly named patterns. Attribution by Oglebay Institute.

BEADED OVALS IN SAND (Figure 408)
See notes in Book 2, pg. 18 concerning this pattern's history. A tumbler has been seen in opalescent green, and a sauce in opalescent white, so it can now be confirmed that this pattern had opalescent production in table pieces.

BEADED SWAG (Figure 409) (See notes on page 16)

BELLAIRE BASKETWEAVE (Figure 410)
Maker: Bellaire Goblet Company **Y.O.P.:** circa 1890 **Colors made:** crystal, amber & blue **Items made:** I can only document the cruet set on matching tray (see Fig. 465), a smaller cruet (shown here) and a toothpick which has identical pattern characteristics, but dates much later (circa 1900) **Repro's:** none **Name by:** *Sm Fin*, pg. 50.

BELMONT DIAMOND (Figure 411)
Maker: Belmont Glass Co., Bellaire, Ohio **Y.O.P.:** circa 1885 **Colors made:** crystal & amber—rare in blue **Items made:** only the cruet was shown in the catalogue I studied **Repro's:** none **Name by:** *Author.*

BELMONT'S REFLECTING FANS (Figure 412)
Maker: Belmont Glass, Bellaire, Ohio **Y.O.P.:** circa 1885 **Colors made:** crystal, amber, blue—rare in canary **Items made:** only the cruet known **Repro's:** none **Name by:** *Author* **Note:** Murray incorrectly calls this *Blockade*, which is a very similar pattern, but not the same one at all.

BEATTY HONEYCOMB (Figure 413)
See pattern notes on page 16 for information on this pattern. The cruet would be very rare in opalescent blue.

BLOCK, FOSTORIA (Figure 414)
Maker: Fostoria's #2574 **Y.O.P.:** reportedly introduced in 1939—discontinued 1966 **Items made:** considerable variety **Name by:** Author **Note:** Many of these cruets are found souvenir dated quite early, which has caused confusion concerning its date of origin.

BLOCK, COOP'S (Figure 415)
Maker: Cooperative Flint Glass **Y.O.P.:** circa 1889 **Colors made:** crystal and ruby-stained **Items made:** everything except toothpick, syrup, and possibly salt shaker **Repro's:** none **Name by:** *Kamm 5*, pg. 93 **Note:** the cruet shown here is previously unlisted.

BRAZILLIAN (Figure 416)
Maker: Fostoria Glass, Moundsville, W. Va. **Y.O.P.:** circa 1901 **Colors made:** crystal and emerald green **Items made:** every shape

(continued on page 92)

420	421	422	423	424	425	426
AISY & BUTTON (n.o.s.)	**DAISY & BUTTON, PANELLED** (n.o.s.)	**DICE & BLOCK** (o.s.)	**DUCHESS** (o.s.)	**ESTHER** (o.s.)	**FLORA** (o.s.)	**FINECUT, HEAVY** (n.o.s.)

427	428	429	430	431	432	433
INECUT, HEAVY (o.s.) (ketchup)	**FLORETTE** (o.s.)	**HICKMAN** (o.s.)	**HOBB'S BLOCK** (o.s.)	**HOBNAIL, FROSTED RUBINA** (n.o.s.)	**I.O.U.** (small)	**I.O.U.** (regular)

DAISY & BUTTON (Figure 420)
Maker: Duncan Glass **Y.O.P.:** circa 1888 **Colors made:** crystal, amber, blue & canary **Items made:** See pg. 75 **Repro's:** not in this shaped cruet **Name by:** Popular nomenclature.

DAISY & BUTTON, PANELLED (Figure 421)
Maker: George Duncan & Sons, with production continued by U.S. Glass after 1891 **Y.O.P.:** circa 1890 **Colors made:** crystal, vaseline, blue and amber-stained (the latter known as *Amberette)* **Items made:** a considerable table service—including a pickle caster insert, salt shakers (no syrup or toothpick known) **Repro's:** none **Name by:** *Kamm 1*, pg. 80 **NOTE:** This cruet in amber-stained would be rare—take care to avoid confusing this pattern with the very similar "Clover" pattern (almost identical in certain pieces). See pg. 72.

DICE & BLOCK (Figure 422)
Maker: Belmont Glass Co. **Y.O.P.:** circa 1885 **Colors made:** crystal, amber, blue, canary **Items made:** cruet only **Repro's:** none **Name by:** *Murray*, Bk. 1, "Cruets Only."

DUCHESS (Figure 423)
Maker: Probably Riverside **Y.O.P.:** circa 1900 **Colors made:** crystal, emerald green, amethyst-flashed crystal (with satin panels), and limited opalescent production (see Book 2, Fig. 200) **Items made:** see listing Book 2 **Repro's:** none **Name by:** *Author* **Note:** Attribution based on the extreme similarity in stoppers between Figs. 423 & 424, and other clues.

ESTHER (Figure 424)
Maker: Riverside **Y.O.P.:** circa 1898 **Colors made:** crystal, emerald green, ruby-stained, amber-stained **Items made:** water set, table set, berry set, cruet (2 sizes), salt shaker, toothpick, cheese dish, 4-

bottle revolving caster set, cake set, pickle tray, celery vase, goblet, jelly compote, covered jam jar, oil lamps **Repro's:** none **Name by:** Orig. mfr. name.

FLORA (Figure 425)
Maker: Beaumont Glass **Y.O.P.:** circa 1896 **Colors made:** see Book 2 for further historical data **Note:** See the reprint from the original Beaumont catalogue on page 63.

FINECUT, HEAVY (Figures 426-427)
Maker: Duncan & Sons **Y.O.P.:** circa 1885 **Colors made:** crystal, amber, blue, canary, possibly apple green **Items made:** too numerous to mention—no toothpick (except hat novelties) known **Repro's:** none to my knowledge **Name by:** Variation of Lee by Author **NOTE:** I am calling these cruets "Heavy Finecut" because they are not exactly the same pattern shown in Kamm, Metz & Lee as "Fine-cut"—the pattern more resembles "Sequoia" (Metz 1, #1807), a variant of *Finecut*. See ad reprint page 71.

FLORETTE (Figure 428)
See notes on page 25 for historical data. The cruet is very hard to find.

HICKMAN (Figure 429)
Maker: McKee & Brothers, Pittsburgh **Y.O.P.:** circa 1897 **Colors made:** crystal, green and ruby-stained **Items made:** every shape imaginable, including miniature toy sets **Repro's:** none **Name by:** *Millard.*

HOBB'S BLOCK (Figure 430)
Maker: Hobbs **Y.O.P.:** circa 1890 **Colors made:** crystal, amber-stained top, frosted with amber top **Items made:** considerable serv-

(continued on page 92)

434	435	436	437	438	439	440
IDYLL (o.s.)	**IVY SCROLL** (n.o.s.)	**LEAF MEDALLION** (o.s.)	**LOCKET ON CHAIN** (o.s.?)	**LOUIS XV** (o.s.)	**MICHIGAN** (o.s.)	**MILLARD** (n.o.s.)

441	442	443	444	445	446	447
MISSOURI (o.s.)	**NAIL** (o.s.)	**OHARA DIAMOND** (o.s.)	**PETTICOAT** (o.s.)	**PINEAPPLE & FAN, HEISY** (n.o.s.)	**PRESSED SWIRL** (n.o.s.)	**PRIZE** (n.o.s.)

IDYLL (Figure 434)
See Book 2 for data concerning this pattern. See ad reprint page 62.

IVY SCROLL (Figure 435)
Maker: Unknown (further research pending) **Y.O.P.:** circa 1900 **Colors made:** crystal, apple green and blue with gold-decorated vines **Items made:** I know of the table set, berry set, water set, cruet, toothpick, and jelly compote—although the pattern is very rarely seen **Repro's:** none **Name by:** *Author* **NOTE:** The Mighell toothpick book calls this *Duncan's 2000*, but it is obviously not the same.

LEAF MEDALLION (Figure 436)
Maker: H. Northwood & Co. **Y.O.P.:** circa 1904 **Colors made:** crystal, green (very dark), deep amethyst, cobalt blue **Items made:** water set, table set, berry set, cruet set (cruet, salt & pepper on matching tray), jelly compote—a toothpick has been reported to me, but will not be documented until I see a photo of same **Repro's:** none **Name by:** *Kamm 5*, pg. 122 **Original name:** Northwood's "Regent." **NOTE:** Avoid confusing this with Metz's pattern with the same name (Bk. 2).

LOCKET ON CHAIN (Figure 437)
Maker: A. H. Heisey & Co. **Y.O.P.:** circa 1897 **Colors made:** primarily crystal—rare in green, vaseline, opal & ruby-stained **Items made:** complete table service — no syrup known **Repro's:** none **Name by:** *Kamm 2*, pg. 57 **NOTE:** The cruet shown here is literally a museum piece.

LOUIS XV (Figure 438)
Maker: Northwood Glass Works **Y.O.P.:** circa 1899 **Colors made:**

emerald green, custard glass—possibly crystal **Items made:** water set, table set, berry set (banana boat shaped), cruet, salt shakers **Repro's:** the sugar bowl is reproduced in purple slag, other colors **Name by:** Orig. Mfr. name.

MICHIGAN (Figure 439)
Maker: A "state series" pattern #15077 of the U.S. Glass Co. **Y.O.P.:** beginning in 1893—continued production for several years **Colors made:** crystal, rose-flashed (maiden's blush), yellow-flashed, blue-stained, and ruby-stained **Items made:** every shape imaginable **Repro's:** the toothpick has been reproduced in many colors **Name by:** orig. mfr. name **Other name:** *Loop & Pillar* (Millard).

MILLARD (Figure 440)
Maker: U.S. Glass #15016 pattern **Y.O.P.:** circa 1895 **Colors made:** crystal, ruby and amber-stained—often etched **Items made:** complete table service **Repro's:** none **Name by:** *Lee*.

MISSOURI (Figure 441)
Maker: U.S. Glass Co. #15058 **Y.O.P.:** circa 1892 **Colors made:** crystal and emerald green, often with gold **Items made:** a limited table service—no toothpick or syrup known **Repro's:** none **Name by:** orig. mfr. name **NOTE:** Kamm reports this pattern was made in blue, canary & amethyst, although these colors have not been documented in my research. Perhaps she means amethyst-flashed, which is possible.

NAIL (Figure 442)
Maker: Originally by Bryce Brothers, with the majority of produc-

56

(continued on page 92)

448
SAXON
(o.s.)

449
SHELL
(o.s.)

450
SPEARPOINT BAND
(n.o.s.)

451
SHOESHONE
(o.s.)

452
TACOMA
(n.o.s.)

453
1000 EYE
(o.s.)

454
1000 EYE,
THREE-KNOB
(o.s.)

455
TRUNCATED CUBE
(o.s.)

456
U.S. RIB
(o.s.)

457
X-RAY
(o.s.)

458
ZENITH
(o.s.)

SAXON (Figure 448)
Maker: Adams & Co., with majority of production after U.S. Glass merger **Y.O.P.:** circa 1890-1895 **Colors made:** crystal & ruby-stained **Items made:** complete table service **Repro's:** none **Name by:** Orig. Mfr. name **NOTE:** The stopper shown in this cruet **is** original—Adams used that same stopper in several of its cruets, despite the fact that they resembled the cruets so little.

SHELL (Figure 449)
Maker: H. Northwood & Co. **Y.O.P.:** circa 1903 **Colors made:** see listing Book 2 **Items made:** see listing Book 2 **Repro's:** none **Name by:** *Kamm 7*, pg. 58 **NOTE:** The stopper shown here is original. Because this stopper is the same used on *S-Repeat*, this brings up the possibility that this is a Northwood-Dugan pattern. However, the later carnival production of *Shell* includes many pieces with Northwood trademarks, so Mr. Northwood apparently retained the molds when he moved to Wheeling. The cruet is rare in opalescent—more often seen in plain colors.

SPEARPOINT BAND (Figure 450)
Maker: McKee at Jeannette, Pa. **Y.O.P.:** circa 1900 **Colors made:** crystal & ruby-stained **Items made:** complete table service **Repro's:** none **Name by:** *Kamm 7*, pg. 31 **Original name:** Gothic **NOTE:** I incorrectly attributed this pattern to U.S. Glass (Duncan) because their Button Arches pattern is frequently found with the same frosted band seen on the cruet shown above. Perhaps McKee copied Duncan, or an independent decorator stocked both patterns. Many answers will never be known.

SHOESHONE (Figure 451)
Maker: My guess from Book 1 turns out to be right—this is U.S. Glass #15046 pattern **Y.O.P.:** circa 1895 **Colors made:** crystal, ruby-stained and emerald green **Items made:** complete table service **Repro's:** absolutely none **Name by:** *BARR*, plt. 12 **Original name:** *Victor* **Other name:** *Blazing Pinwheels* **NOTE:** Take care not to confuse this with the very similar "Sterling" (or *Pinwheels*), also made in ruby-stained glass. *Shoeshone* has a diamond within a diamond—*Sterling* does not.

TACOMA (Figure 452)
Maker: Originally by Greensburg Glass, circa 1894, with continued production by Model Flint Glass, Albany, Ind. in 1900 **Colors made:** crystal, ruby-stained, amber-stained, limited amber & green **Items made:** complete table service **Repro's:** none **NOTE:** The original stopper to this cruet was a pressed faceted non-pattern stopper. Two sizes of syrups were made—called a syrup (short) & molasses (tall).

THOUSAND EYE—2 VARIANTS (Figures 453-454)
Maker: Figure 453 was made by Richards & Hartley—Figure 454 was made by Adams & Co. **Y.O.P.:** circa 1890 with continued production of both by U.S. Glass **Colors made:** crystal, amber, vaseline, blue and apple green—Fig. 454 also made in white opalescent **Items made:** too numerous to mention—every shape imaginable **Repro's:** yes, but not exactly as shown here (the repro's are shaped differently) **Name by:** *LEE EAPG*, plt. 137.

TRUNCATED CUBE (Figure 455)
Maker: Thompson Glass Co. #77 pattern, Uniontown, Pa. **Y.O.P.:** beginning in 1892 **Colors made:** crystal & ruby-stained **Items made:** complete table service—a syrup would be rare **Repro's:** none **Name by:** *Millard* **NOTE:** In certain pieces, this pattern is confused for *Sunk Honeycomb*.

(continued on page 92)

Cruet Sets

(text next page)

459
LOG & STAR
(o.s.)

460
NESTOR
(o.s.)

461
CHRYSANTHEMUM SPRIG
(n.o.s.)

462
DOUBLE CIRCLE
(o.s.)

463
JEWELLED HEART
(o.s.)

464
**FORGET-ME-NOT,
CHALLINOR'S**
(o.s.)

465
BELLAIRE BASKETWEAVE
(o.s.)

466
S-REPEAT
(o.s.)

467
STARS & BARS
(o.s.)

468
TINY OPTIC
(o.s.)

469
SCALLOPED SKIRT
(o.s.)

470
CROESUS
(o.s.)

LOG & STAR (Figure 459)
Maker: Bellaire Goblet Co., with production continued by U.S. Glass (#373 pattern)   **Y.O.P.:** circa 1890-1892   **Colors made:** crystal, amber and 2 shades of blue   **Items made:** limited service—no toothpick, syrup known   **Repro's:** none   **Other name:** *Cube & Diamond* (Lee)
IMPORTANT NOTE: There are 2 different size cruets with 2 different stoppers. Note that the patterns on the salt, pepper & tray differ slightly from the cruet—in fact this other pattern is called Milton, and the differences in the two patterns are so slight, it makes me wonder that they were not meant to be the same pattern originally—the cruet set (which is original) seems to confirm this theory.

NESTOR (Figure 460)
Maker: The Northwood Company, while under the control of the National Glass Co.   **Y.O.P.:** 1903   **Colors made:** blue, apple green and amethyst, frequently beautifully decorated   **Items made:** Table set, water set, berry set, toothpick, cruet, salt & pepper, jelly compote, cruet set on tray (2 trays known, one in the *Chrysanthemum Sprig* pattern)   **Repro's:** none   **Name by:** Orig. name from 1903 Wards catalogue.   **NOTE:** The tray shown above is signed Northwood in script—this set is seldom found decorated.

CHRYSANTHEMUM SPRIG (Figure 461)
Maker: The Northwood Company, Indiana, Pa.   **Y.O.P.:** circa 1898, ten years later than I was earlier led to believe   **Colors made:** custard and blue opaque (called blue custard, which is a misnomer)   **Items made:** water set, table set, berry set (banana boat shaped), cruet, salt & pepper, toothpick, jelly compote, celery vase (rare), condiment tray   **Repro's:** new toothpicks not in original colors   **Name by:** *Kamm 3*, pg. 159   **Note:** The cruet, salt & pepper do not fit onto the tray well at all—it seems unlikely that it would be used to hold just the salt, pepper and *toothpick*. The stopper in the cruet is a plastic reproduction which recently appeared on the market. They are light in weight, and are a very good copy in color—so BEWARE!

DOUBLE CIRCLE (Figure 462)
Maker: Jefferson Glass Co.   **Y.O.P.:** circa 1902   **Colors made:** crystal, sapphire blue and apple green   **Items made:** only made in the cruet set shown above   **Repro's:** none   **Name by:** *Pet Sal*, pg. 156-R.

JEWELLED HEART (Figure 463)
See page 29 for notes concerning this pattern.

FORGET-ME-NOT, CHALLINOR'S (Figure 464)
See page 18 for notes concerning this pattern.

BELLAIR BASKETWEAVE (Figure 465)
See page 54 for notes concerning this pattern.

S-REPEAT (Figure 466)
See page 41 for notes concerning this pattern.

STARS & BARS (Figure 467)
Maker: Bellaire Goblet Company   **Y.O.P.:** circa 1890 with production possibly continued by U.S. Glass after 1891   **Colors made:** crystal, amber & blue—rare in vaseline   **Items made:** complete service, including miniatures and a night lamp   **Repro's:** none known   **Name by:** *Kamm 1*, pg. 64   **Other name:** *Daisy & Cube* (by Lee, who seemed to ignore Kamm names).

TINY OPTIC (Figure 468)
Maker: Probably Jefferson Glass   **Y.O.P.:** circa 1905-1910   **Colors made:** crystal, amethyst, blue, green and custard glass   **Items made:** complete table service—the custard had quite limited production, but is not very desirable to custard collectors because it is so plain.   **Repro's:** None   **Name by:** *Author*—see Book 1   **NOTE:** The cloverleaf tray to this cruet set has a hobnail motif on the base, and is identical to the one right next to it.

SCALLOPED SKIRT (Figure 469)
Maker: Because of the matching stopper and tray, now known to be Jefferson Glass Co.   **Y.O.P.:** circa 1905   **Colors made:** crystal, amethyst, apple green & blue—always enamel decorated   **Items made:** table set, water set, berry set, cruet set, toothpick   **Repro's:** none   **Name by:** Mighell (Toothpick Holders)   **NOTE:** I incorrectly attributed this as "possibly Northwood" in Book 1.

CROESUS (Figure 470)
Maker: Riverside   **Y.O.P.:** circa 1897   **Colors made:** crystal, amethyst, emerald green, all usually with gold   **Items made:** water set, table set, berry set, cruet (2 sizes), salt shaker, celery vase, toothpick, jelly compote, breakfast creamer & sugar, tray for small cruet set, tray for large cruet set (shown here), 2 sizes of plates   **Repro's:** new toothpicks in **all** original colors, new tumblers by Mosser, and a reported new table set from Japan in all original colors   **Name by:** Orig. mfr. name.

(continued from page 51)

ACORN DIAMONDS (Figure 388)
Maker: U.S. Glass Company's Factory B (Bryce)   **Y.O.P.:** circa 1891   **Colors made:** crystal, amber & blue known   **Items made:** only the syrup is shown in the catalogue (see page 78)—no other items in the pattern documented   **Repro's:** none   **Name by:** *Author.*

FLOWER MOLD (Figure 389)
See pattern notes on page 25.

INVERTED THUMBPRINT (Figure 390)
See pattern notes on page 28.

LIBBEY'S MAIZE (Figure 391)
See pattern notes on page 32. Shown here is the decorated opal.

QUILTED PHLOX (Figure 392)
See pattern notes on page 37. Shown here is a luscious pink opaque which highly resembles pink slag with its swirls of white.

RIBBED OPAL LATTICE (Figure 393)
See pattern notes on page 38. This tall version of the sugar shaker is by no means rare—just thought it should be shown for comparison with the shorter, rarer version shown as Figure 251.

RIDGE SWIRL (Figure 394)
See pattern notes on page 38.

ROPE & RIBS (Figure 394)
Maker: Central Glass Co., Wheeling, W. Va.   **Y.O.P.:** circa 1890   **Colors made:** crystal, amber, blue & canary   **Items made:** I have only seen the sugar shaker and creamer to date—further documentation pending   **Repro's:** None   **Name by:** *Author.*

ROPE & THUMBPRINT (Figures 395-397)
Maker: Central Glass Company, Wheeling, W. Va.   **Y.O.P.:** circa 1885   **Colors made:** crystal, amber, blue & canary   **Items made:** considerable table service—no toothpick or cruet was made   **Repro's:** none   **Name by:** Orig. Mfr. Name (*Revi*)—the name is derived from the twisted rope handle which the creamer and water pitcher have on them. This was Central's #796 pattern.

SUNSET (Figure 398)
See pattern notes on page 43. Shown here is the rare custard.

WILDFLOWER (Figure 399)
See pattern notes on page 46.

COLORATURA (Figures 400-405)
Maker: Hobbs, Brockunier & Co.   **Y.O.P.:** circa 1885   **Items made:** a series of matching sugar shakers in identical shape with identical tops   **Colors made:** shown here—also made in decorated amberina and rubina verde   **Repro's:** none   **Name by:** *Author.*

FIG. #470-B
Rare Ruby-Stained "THE PRIZE"

FIG. #470-A
Rare Amber "WHEAT & BARLEY"

Early Ad & Catalogue Reprints

SYRUP CANS

No. 1030   No. 1008   No. 1009   No. 1031   No. 1032

Reprint from 1901 Fostoria Glass Catalogue.

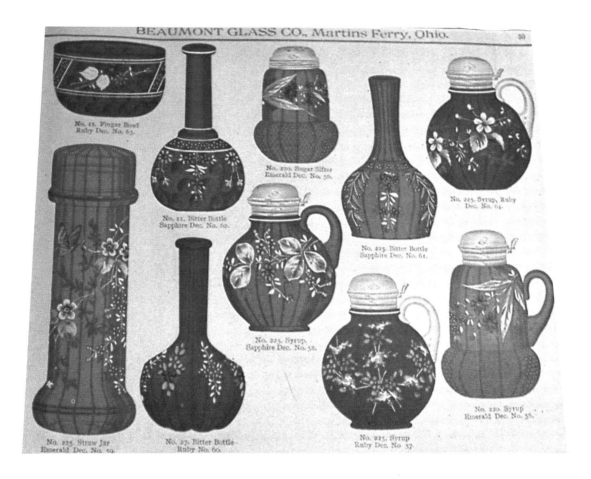

Reprints from Beaumont Glass Co. catalogue, circa 1895

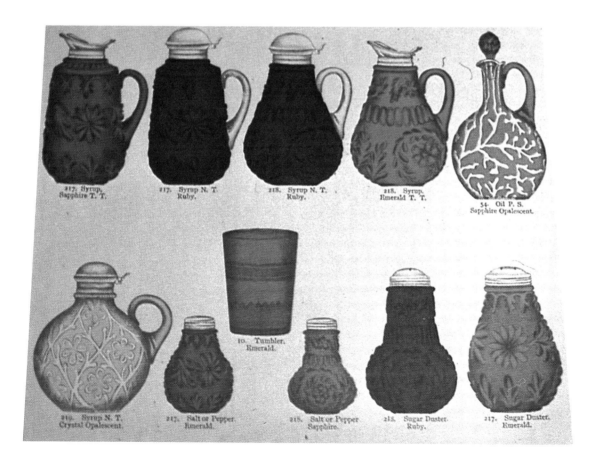

Reprints from Jefferson Glass Co. catalogue, circa 1907

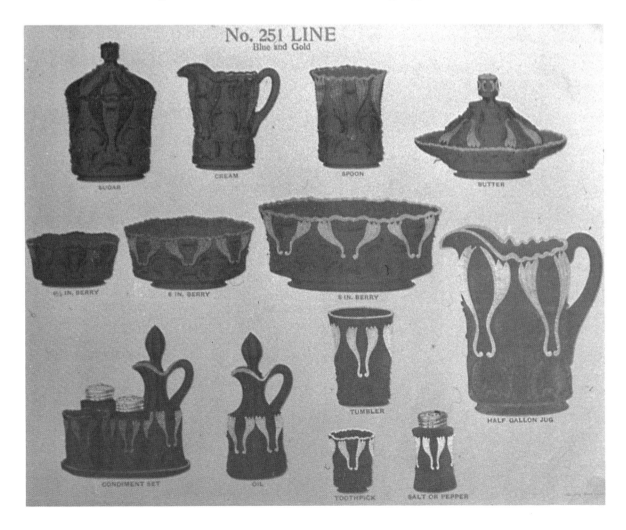

62

Reprints from Beaumont Glass Co. catalogue, circa 1895

Reprints from U.S. Glass factory "C" catalogue (Challinor), 1891 (above) "Banded Shells", rare in pink & blue opaque. (Below) Note the "One-O-One" toothpick at the top left (previously unattributed). The "Little Acorn" salt shaker at top-center is not the same as the "Acorn" on pg. 14.

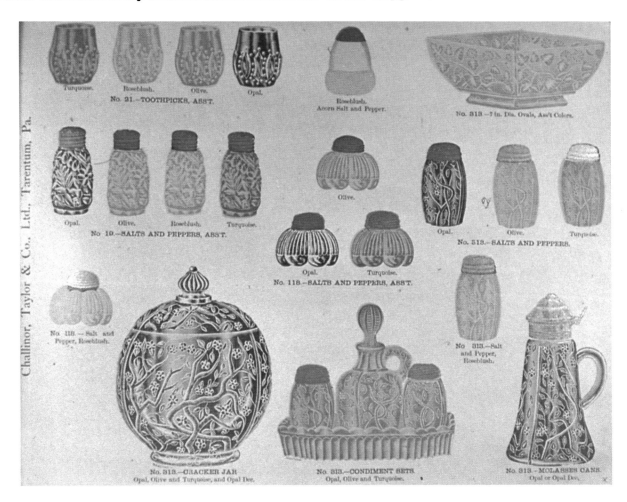

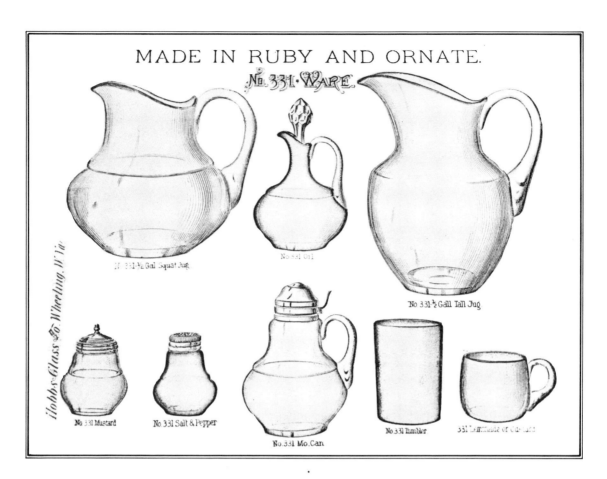

Reprints of 1890 Hobbs Glass Co. catalogue, featuring the "Bulbous Base" pattern—note the term "ruby" was used to describe cranberry.

Reprints from 1885 Hobbs, Brockunier & Co. catalogue—note the
"Daisy & Button" catsup at the bottom right.

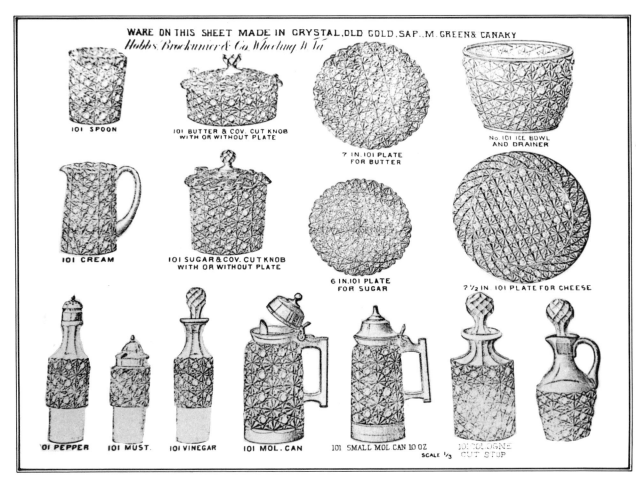

No 4 P.D. DECANTER CUT STOPPER

76 P.D. BAR BOT & STOP CUT

89 OPTIC BAR ENG.D. NO. 263

89 BAR BOTTLE RUBINA VERDE

319-O SUGAR & COV. RUBINA VERDE

309 BITTER RUBINA VERDE

509 LEMON P.D. RUBINA VERDE

507 CUSTARD RUBINA VERDE

98 P.D. MOL CAN 16 OZ

97 P.D. MOL CAN 12 OZ

PD BBL MUSTARD

4 ½ 304 NAPPY RUBINA VERDE

5-304 NAPPY RUBINA VERDE

216 P.D. PEPPER

216 P.D. SALT

225 SALT P.D.

312 P.D. OIL

SUGAR SIFTER RUBY P.D.

101 P.D. WATER SET RUBINA VERDE

Reprints from 1890 Hobbs Glass Co. catalogue. Note the rare "Hobbs' Block" syrup shown below.

Hobbs Glass Co. Wheeling, W.Va.

330-Boat Celery

330 Mol Can Pat Glass Lip.

330-Water Bottle.

330-Tumbler

330-½ Gal Tankard

SCALE ⅛

330-Finger Bowl

U.S. Glass Factory "C" (Columbia Glass at Findlay), 1891 — Display of their Dewdrop line, commonly called Hobnail today (see Figures 143-144, this volume). Note the sugar shaker and mustard mold were the same. Dewdrop was a popular pattern motif, and several other companies had their own variation of this pattern.

U.S. Glass Factory "C" (Columbia), 1891 — Note the scarce syrup shown here (rare in color).

339 Celery
Decorated Nº 25.

339 Spoon.
Decorated Nº 25.

339 Sugar & Cover.
Decorated Nº 25.

339 Butter & Cover.
Decorated Nº 25.

339 Tankard   Decorated Nº 25.

½ SCALE.

U.S. Glass Factory "H" (Hobbs), 1891 — Display of their #339 pattern, or Leaf & Flower (Lee).

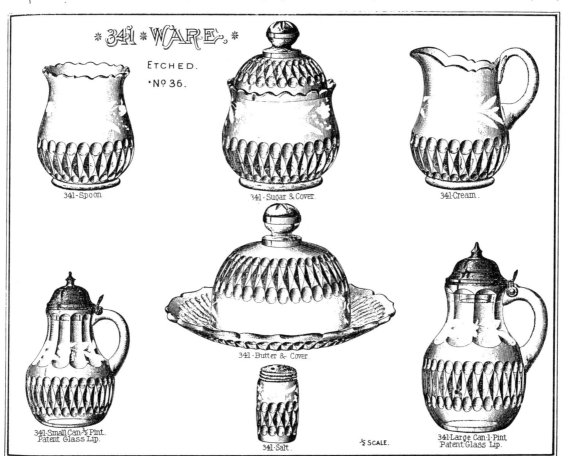

✴ 341 ✴ WARE ✴

ETCHED.
Nº 36.

341 - Spoon.

341 - Sugar & Cover.

341 - Cream.

341 - Butter & Cover.

341 - Salt.

341 - Small Can - ½ Pint.
Patent Glass Lip.

341 - Large Can - 1 Pint.
Patent Glass Lip.

½ SCALE.

U.S. Glass Factory "H" (Hobbs), 1891 — Display of #341 pattern (Mario). See Figure 190, this volume. Note the two sizes of syrups.

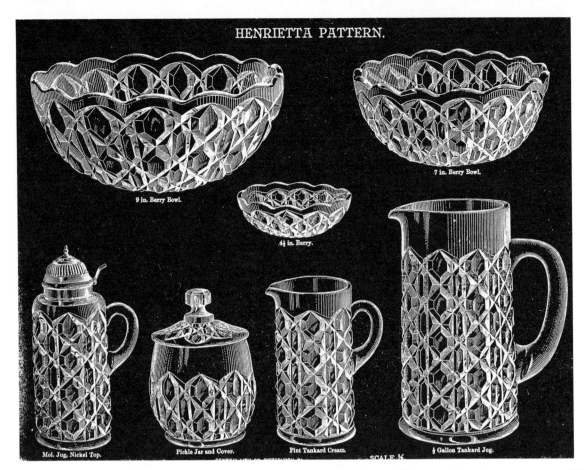

U. S. Glass Factory "C" (Columbia Glass at Findlay), 1891—Display of the true Henrietta pattern, which is extremely rare in ruby-stained glass, for which the much more common Hexagon Block (seen below) is frequently confused. Note the similarities and differences.

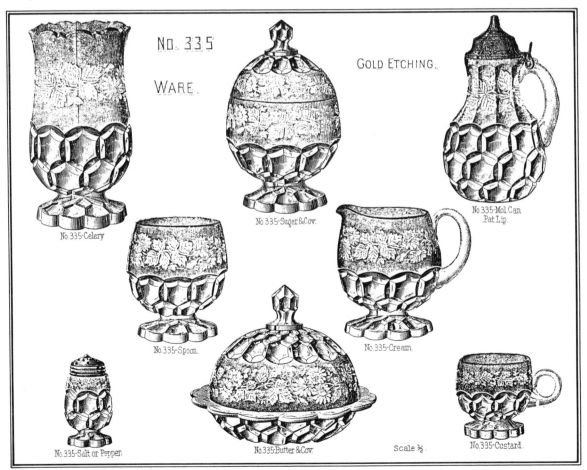

U.S. Glass Factory "H" (Hobbs), circa 1891—display of the Hexagon Block pattern, which is all too often called incorrectly "Henrietta" due to Barretts misnomer in his book on ruby-stained glass. See Figure 131, this book.

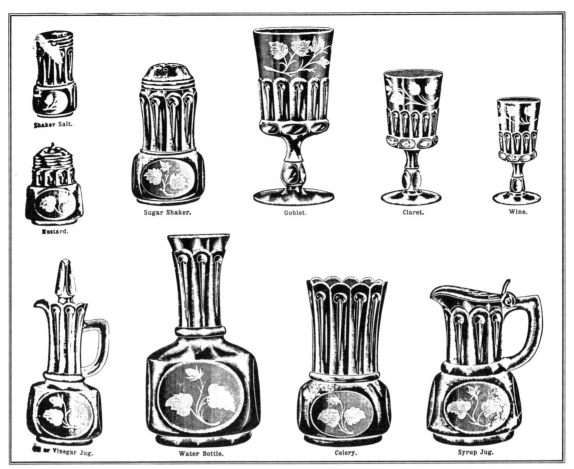

Shaker Salt.

Mustard.

Sugar Shaker.

Goblet.

Claret.

Wine.

or Vinegar Jug.

Water Bottle.

Celery.

Syrup Jug.

U.S. Glass, Factory F (Richards & Hartley)—note the cruet, sugar shaker & syrup—all scarce, but especially in ruby-stained!!

Bag Celery.

9 in. No. 800 Orange Bowl

8 in. No 800 Orange Bowl

BAG WARE
ALSO MADE IN COLORS

7 & 8 in Bag Bowl & Cov.

No 800 Catsup Pressed or Cut Stopper

7 & 8 in Bag Bowl Uncovered

SCALE ½

Duncan & Sons, circa 1890—Note that what is often called a large cruet was actually listed as a "catsup" dispenser—see Figure 427, this book.

71

U.S. Glass, Factory D (Duncan)—display of their "Ellrose" pattern in Amberette stained ware. The same amberette label was used on Duncan's other amber-stained patterns. Note the original stopper to the cruet.

U.S. Glass, Factory F (Richards & Hartley), circa 1891—display of their "Mikado" (today called Daisy & Button with Cross-bar). Note the item most call a large cruet was originally listed as a "ketchup". Note the toothpick which in no way resembles the rest of the set.

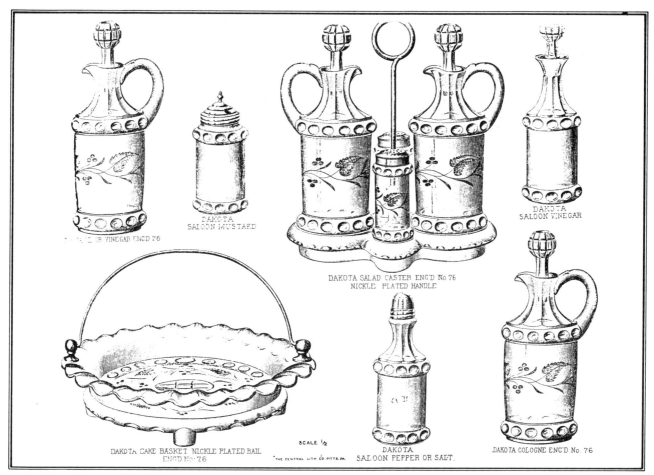

U.S. Glass Factory "F" (Richards & Hartley), circa 1891—Display of the Dakota pattern, including a very rare condiment set. Note the cruet was also listed as a "cologne". This cruet and set would be very rare in ruby-stained.

U.S. Glass Factory "F" (Richards & Hartley)—Display of their #190, Bar & Diamond (Lee) which shows the syrup and sugar shaker, both rare in ruby-stained. This pattern is also known as Kokomo (Millard) and Swirl Band (Kamm).

800 PATTERN.

No800½ Salt Bottle
Plated Top.

No800½ Mustard
Plated Top.

No800½ Pepper Bottle
Plated Top.

4 in Compart.

4½ Nappy.

4 in Nappy.

4½ Berry Nappy.

5 in Cream Nappy.

No800 Pickle Boat

No800 Mol Can.

Pint No800 Mol Can.

No 800 Cheese Plate & Cov.

No800 Table Tumbler

No800 Cordial
1 oz.

No800 Wine
2½ oz.

No800 Claret
4¼ oz.

No800 Champs
6½ oz.

Celery

½ Gall Pitcher

ALSO MADE IN COLORS.

4½ Sled

Ind Salt

No800 Mustard

No800 Salt or
Pepper Bottle

Table Salt

11 in Celery Boat.

6 in Flanged Butter

No800 Goblet
9½ oz.

Goblet

No800 Oil or Vinegar Bottle

½ Gall No800 Tankard.

No. 800 Cheese Plate & Cov.

Duncan's #800 pattern (circa 1890) – the panelled version is often called Heavy Panelled Finecut (Kamm), is sometimes labelled "Georgia" and is not the same as Lee's "Finecut."

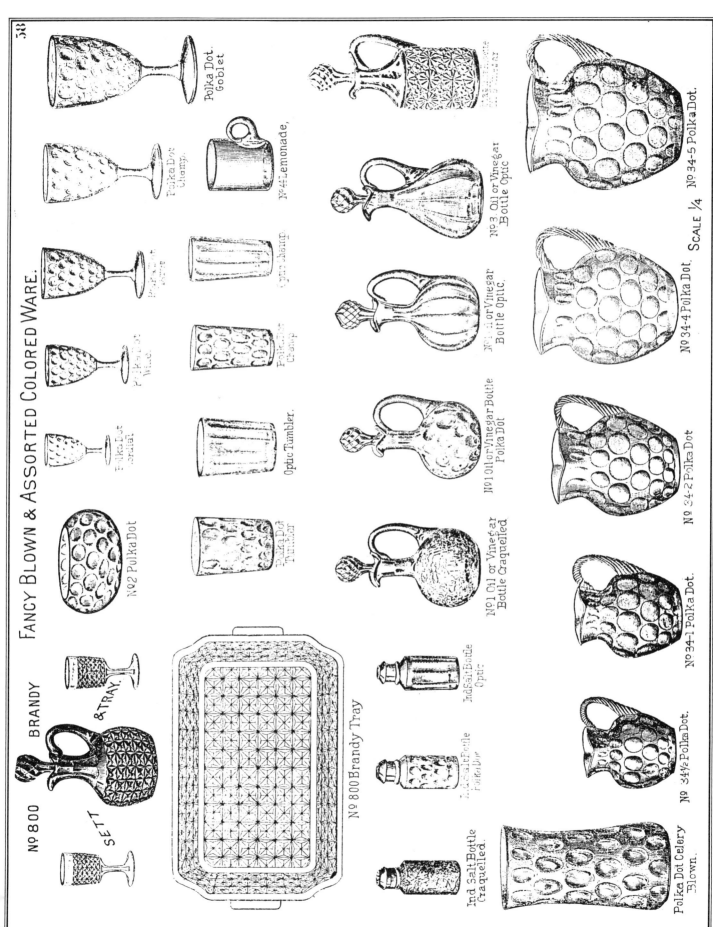

38

FANCY BLOWN & ASSORTED COLORED WARE.

Polka Dot. Goblet

Polka Dot. Champ.

N° 44 Lemonade,

Polka Dot Champ.

Polka Dot. Wine.

Polka Dot. Cordial.

N°2 Polka Dot

Optic Champ.

Polka Dot. Champ.

Optic Tumbler.

Polka Dot. Tumbler.

N°3. Oil or Vinegar Bottle Optic

N° 1 Oil or Vinegar Bottle Optic.

N° 0 Oil or Vinegar Bottle Polka Dot.

N° 1 Oil or Vinegar Bottle Craquelled.

N° 34-5 Polka Dot.

N° 34-4 Polka Dot.

N° 34-2 Polka Dot.

N° 34-1 Polka Dot.

SCALE ¼

BRANDY

&TRAY.

N° 800

SETT

N° 800 Brandy Tray

Ind. Salt Bottle Optic

Ind. Salt Bottle Polka Dot

Ind. Salt Bottle Craquelled.

N° 34½ Polka Dot.

Polka Dot Celery Blown.

Duncan & Sons, circa 1890 (not part of a U.S. Glass catalogue) — note the extreme similarity of the Inverted Thumbprint line to Hobb's line.

75

Wheat & Barley syrups (2 sizes)—from 1891 U.S. Glass catalogue, Factory B (Bryce). Made in crystal, rare in amber & blue. Original name: *Duquesne.*

Hobbs' #324 syrup, circa 1890 —rare in color.

15117—Molasses Can—Gold and Emerald Dots—Gold and Ruby Dots—Gold and Gold Dots. $4.00 per dozen.

15118—Molasses Can—Gold Decorated Tin Top, $2.80 per dozen.

15112—Molasses Can—Gold Decorated
Tin Top, $2.50 per doz.
Patent Tin Top,   2.70   "
Nickel Top,   3.20   "

Syrups from a 1909 U.S. Glass catalogue—(left to right) *Bullseye & Daisy* (rare in green), *#15118* (un-named), *Pattee Cross* (rose-flashed).

No 95 Can Pat T T

128 Can Tin Top

Orient Can P B T

79 Can P T T

Quart Plain Can P B T

U.S. Glass, factory "B" (Bryce)—display of syrups from 1891 catalogue. Top left syrup is in the Beaded Band pattern (Lee), rare in color.

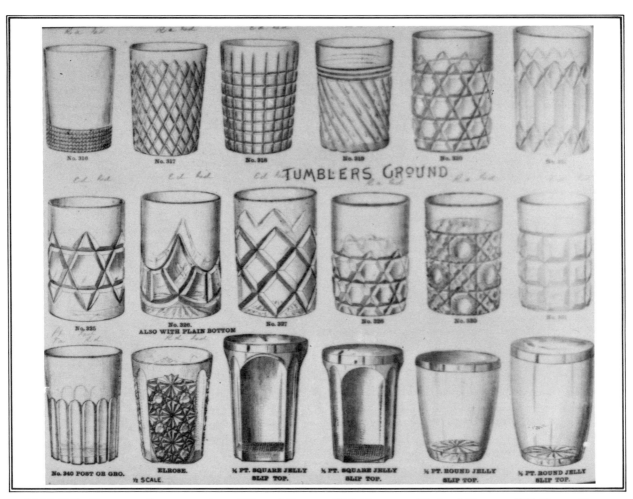

1891 U.S. Glass catalogue reprint—(Above) Factory "D", Duncan; (Below) Factory "B", Bryce Bros.

Syrups from 1909 U.S. Glass catalogue—#15047 (U.S. Colonial) rare in green; #15121 (Portland) primarily clear only; #15082 (Church Windows), rare color-flashed; #15077 (Michigan), rare color stained; #15041 (known as Czarina, Pineapple & Fan or Holbrook), rare ruby-stained; #15099 and #15107, no names, only in crystal.

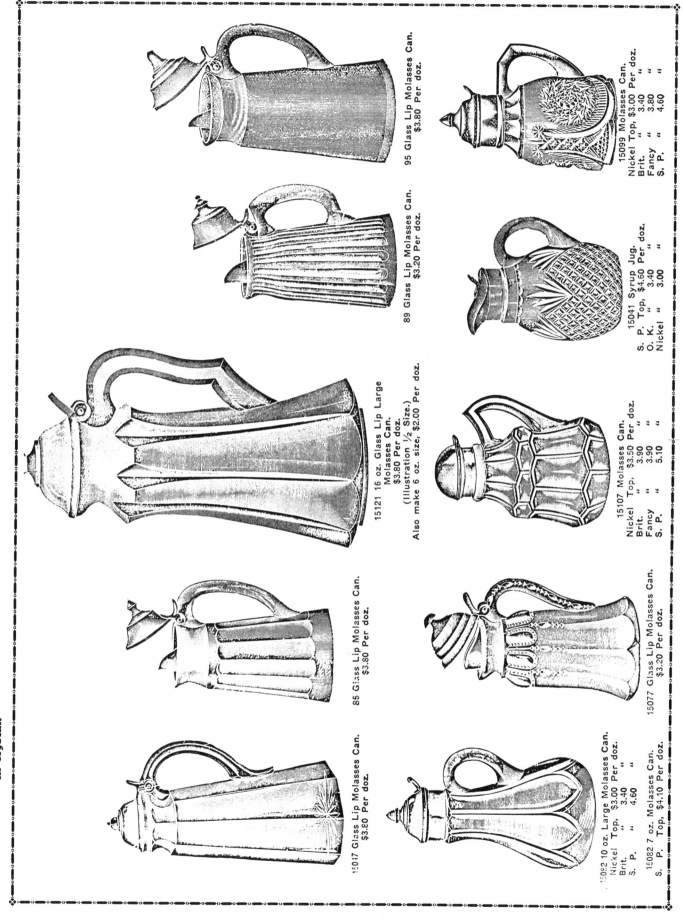

95 Glass Lip Molasses Can.
$3.80 Per doz.

15099 Molasses Can.
Nickel Top, $3.00 Per doz.
Brit.   "   3.40   "
Fancy   "   3.80   "
S. P.   "   4.60   "

89 Glass Lip Molasses Can.
$3.20 Per doz.

15041 Syrup Jug.
S. P. Top, $4.60 Per doz.
O. K.   "   3.40   "
Nickel   "   3.00   "

15121 16 oz. Glass Lip Large
Molasses Can.
$3.80 Per doz.
(Illustration ½ Size.)
Also make 6 oz. size, $2.00 Per doz.

15107 Molasses Can.
Nickel Top, $3.50 Per doz.
Brit.   "   3.90   "
Fancy   "   3.90   "
S. P.   "   5.10   "

85 Glass Lip Molasses Can.
$3.80 Per doz.

15077 Glass Lip Molasses Can.
$3.20 Per doz.

15047 Glass Lip Molasses Can.
$3.20 Per doz.

15082 10 oz. Large Molasses Can.
Nickel Top, $3.00 Per doz.
Brit.   "   3.40   "
S. P.   "   4.60   "

15082 7 oz. Molasses Can.
S. P. Top, $4.10 Per doz.

79

Exerpts from U.S. Glass Co. Catalogues (circa 1908)

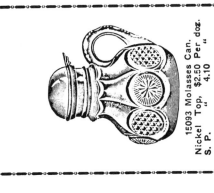

15093 Molasses Can.
Nickel Top, $2.50 Per doz.
S. P. " 4.10 "

The States
(rare in green)

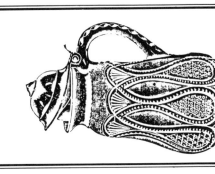

**New Jersey
#15070**
(rare ruby-stained)

15111 Molasses Can.
S. P. Top, $5.10 Per doz.
Brit. " 3.90 "
Fancy " 3.90 "
(Illustration ½ Size.)

**#15111
Primarily crystal**

341 Large Glass Lip Molasses Can.
$3.80 Per doz.

**#341 syrup
crystal only**

▲ 15095 Molasses Can
T. T., $1.30 per doz.
P. T. T., 1.50 "
N. T., 2.20 "

Panelled Palm
(scarce rose-flashed)

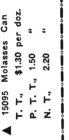

15048 Syrup Jug.
S. P. Top, $4.60 Per doz.
Brit. " 3.40 "
Nickel " 3.00 "

Pennsylvania
(rare in green or
ruby-stained)

▲ 15091 Molasses Can
7 oz.
N. T., $2.50 per doz.
O. K. T., 2.90 "

Arched Ovals
(rare green or
ruby-stained)

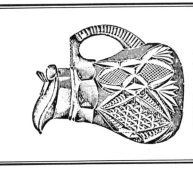

15086 7 oz. Molasses Can.
S. P. Top, $4.10 Per doz.
Nickel " 2.50 "

15086 10 oz. Molasses Can.
S. P. Top, $4.60 Per doz.
Brit. " 3.40 "
Nickel " 3.00 "

**Virginia (Galloway)
Primarily crystal**

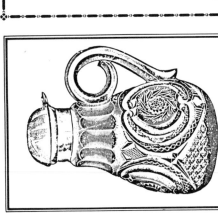

▲ 15084 Molasses Can
N. T., $2.50 per doz.
O. K. T., 2.90 "

New Hampshire
(rare rose-flashed)

15104 Molasses Can.
Nickel Top, $3.50 Per doz.
Brit. " 3.90 "
Fancy " 3.90 "
S. P. " 5.10 "

**#15104
Primarily crystal**

Sugar Sifter.

Molasses Can.

Four oz. Oil.

**Factory
(Richards & Hartley)
Assortment of
"Block & Fan"
(made in crystal,
ruby-stained & opal.)**

No. 335 Molasses Can—Plated Top.
Ewer Mouth.

No. 335 Sugar Sifter—N. T.

**Factory D
(Duncan & Sons)
"Beaded Swirl"
(Very rare in emerald green)**

**Factory D
(Duncan & Sons)
"Late Block"
(Rare in ruby-stained)**

331 SUGAR SIFTER.

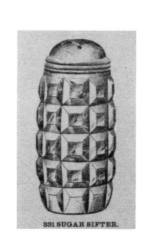

No. 331—HOTEL MOL. CAN EWER,
MOUTH PLATED.

Syrup Jug.

Factory A
"Fleur-de-lis & Tassle"
(This syrup rare in green)

Oil or Vinegar Jug.

Factory D (Duncan)
"Barred Ovals"
(A scarce cruet in ruby-stain)

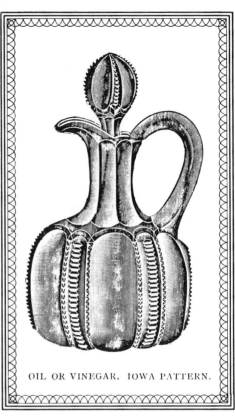

OIL OR VINEGAR. IOWA PATTERN.

Factory Unknown
"Iowa" State Pattern
(Made in rose-flashed)

No.26 Mol Can Dec No 144

Factory C
"Challinor's #26"
(Decorated milk glass)

SYRUP JUG.

"Saxon" Syrup
(Rare in ruby-stained)
(Factory A)

VINEGAR OR OIL JUG.

Saxon Cruet
(Scarce in ruby-stained)
(Note original stopper. Figure 448)

Syrup Jug.

Oil or Vinegar Jug.

(cruet—note orig. stopper)

▲ Factory A—Adams & Co. ▶
"Crystal Wedding"
(These two would be rare
in ruby-stained)

Tarentum's "Royal Crystal"
(A rare cruet in ruby-stained) ▶
(Note the misnomer)

Large Molasses Can.

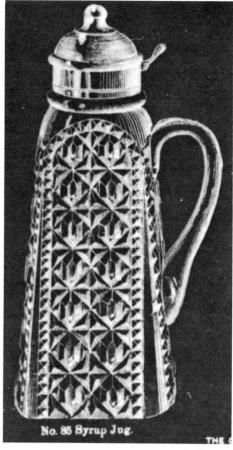

No. 85 Syrup Jug.

Valencia Waffle—Factory "A"
(Adams & Co., #85 pattern)

Syrup Jug.

▲ Factory A—Adams & Co. ▶
"Hidalgo"
(These would be rare
in ruby-stained)

Shaker Sugar.

Factory B (Bryce Brothers)
Floral Diamond Band—#900

83

Eagle Glass & Mfg. Co.
(Unnamed Pattern)

Molasses Can; Tin Top.

"Feather"
(McKee & Bros.)
circa 1895

Molasses Can.

"Cut Block"
(A. H. Heisey Co.)
circa 1900
very rare in ruby-stained

1031.—SYRUP.

Fostoria's "Wild Rose"

1032.—SYRUP.

Fostoria's "Weeping Roses"

Oil.

Jewelled Moon & Star
(Co-operative Flint Glass Co.)
circa 1900

Wedding Bells
(Fostoria Glass Co.)
circa 1901

OIL BOTTLE.
RIBBON PATTERN.

Cambridge Glass Co.
"Bridal Rosette" Cruet
circa 1908

Eagle Glass & Manufacturing Co.,
Wellsburg, W. Va.,

No. 75 Sugar Sifter.

No. 100 Molasses Can.

No. 45 Tooth Pick.

MANUFACTURERS AND GLASS DECORATORS.

Seven-inch Shade Lamps and Night Lamps a specialty.   Decorated Salts and Peppers, Sugar, Sifters, Molasses Cans, Etc., Etc.   Also Opal Blanks for Decorating.   OPAL NEST EGGS.   Write for Catalogues and Prices.

PRIVATE MOLDS A SPECIALTY, FOR BLOWN AND PRESSED OPAL GOODS.

Sample Room at Monongahela House, Room 159.
Representative, S. O. Paull.

MOLASSES POT,
EAGLE GLASS & M'F'G CO.

**Unnamed Pattern
(From 1901 Ad)**

1001. Shaker Salt.

1007. Molasses Can.

1002. Shaker Salt.

**Aug. 1901 Ad from
National Glass Co.
(operating the Lancaster
Glass Works,
Lancaster, O.)**

MOLASSES CAN.
THE EAGLE GLASS & MFG. CO.

**Unnamed Pattern
(From 1901 Ad)**

Sugar Sifters.

ESTABLISHED 1861.

No. 447. Sugar, Decorated.

No. 411. Sugar, Decorated Bisque.

No. 418. Sugar. Green, Turquoise and Opal.

Send for Prices.

GILLINDER & SONS, Inc.,

135 Oxford Street, - - PHILADELPHIA.

1897 Ad from "China, Glass & Lamps"

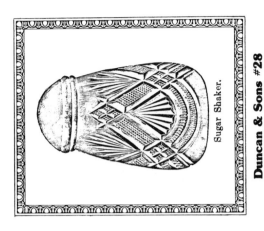

Sugar Shaker.

Duncan & Sons #28

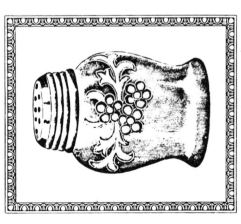

Eagle Glass & Mfg. Co.
(circa 1901)

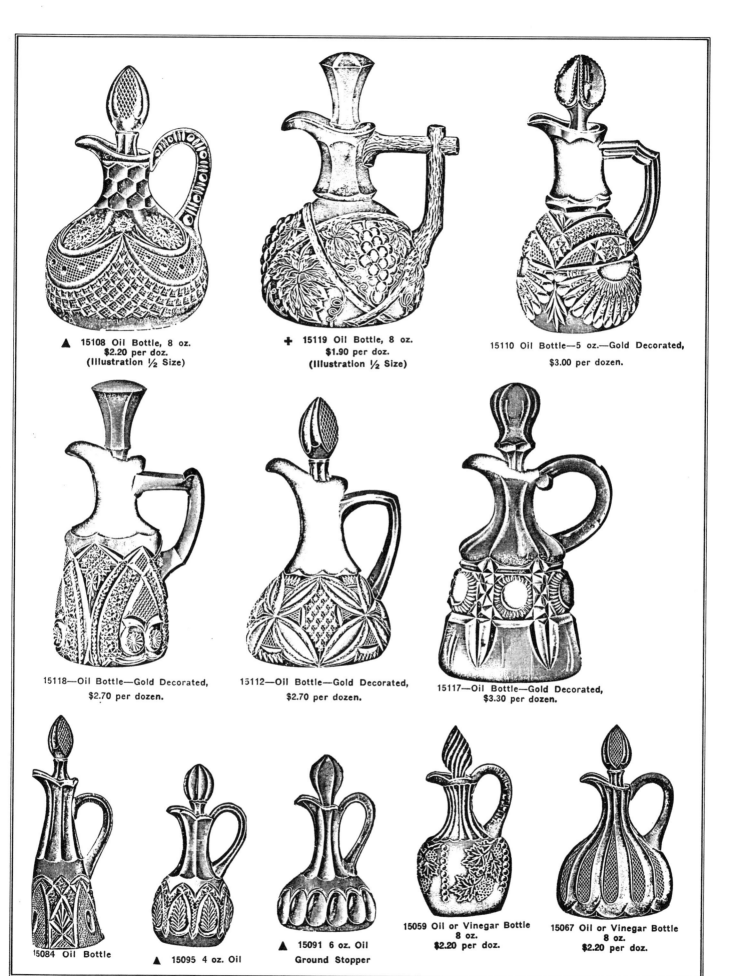

▲ 15108 Oil Bottle, 8 oz.
$2.20 per doz.
(Illustration ½ Size)

✝ 15119 Oil Bottle, 8 oz.
$1.90 per doz.
(Illustration ½ Size)

15110 Oil Bottle—5 oz.—Gold Decorated,
$3.00 per dozen.

15118—Oil Bottle—Gold Decorated,
$2.70 per dozen.

15112—Oil Bottle—Gold Decorated,
$2.70 per dozen.

15117—Oil Bottle—Gold Decorated,
$3.30 per dozen.

15084 Oil Bottle

▲ 15095 4 oz. Oil

▲ 15091 6 oz. Oil
Ground Stopper

15059 Oil or Vinegar Bottle
8 oz.
$2.20 per doz.

15067 Oil or Vinegar Bottle
8 oz.
$2.20 per doz.

Cruets From 1909 U.S. Glass Catalogue

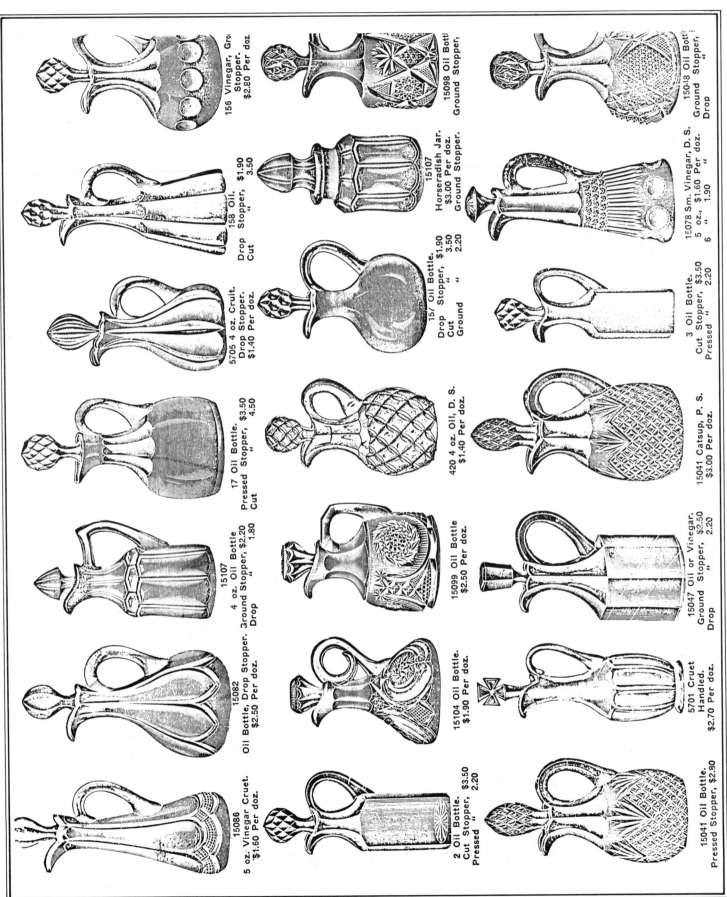

156 Vinegar, Ground Stopper. $2.80 Per doz.

15098 Oil Bottle, Ground Stopper,

15048 Oil Bottle, Ground Stopper, Drop

158 Oil. Stopper, $1.90 Drop " 3.50 Cut

15107 Horseradish Jar. $3.00 Per doz. Ground Stopper.

15078 Sm. Vinegar, D. S. 5 oz., $1.60 Per doz. 6 " 1.90

5705 4 oz. Cruit. Drop Stopper. $1.40 Per doz.

15/ Oil Bottle. Drop Stopper, $1.90 Cut " 3.50 Ground " 2.20

3 Oil Bottle. Cut Stopper, $3.50 Pressed " 2.20

17 Oil Bottle. Pressed Stopper, $3.50 Cut " 4.50

420 4 oz. Oil, D. S. $1.40 Per doz.

15041 Catsup, P. S. $3.00 Per doz.

15107 4 oz. Oil Bottle Ground Stopper, $2.20 Drop " 1.80

15099 Oil Bottle $2.50 Per doz.

15047 Oil or Vinegar. Ground Stopper, $2.50 Drop " 2.20

15082 Oil Bottle, Drop Stopper. $2.50 Per doz.

15104 Oil Bottle. $1.90 Per doz.

5701 Cruet Handled. $2.70 Per doz.

15086 5 oz. Vinegar Cruet. $1.60 Per doz.

2 Oil Bottle. Cut Stopper, $3.50 Pressed " 2.20

15041 Oil Bottle. Pressed Stopper, $2.80

Display of cruets from 1909 U.S. Glass catalogue, many available only in crystal. Note the original stoppers

Reprints from Beaumont Glass Co. catalogue, circa 1895.
Note the rare salt & pepper (2 different shapes) & cruet set.

MORE ADDITIONS AND CORRECTIONS TO BOOK I

ADDITIONS AND CORRECTIONS TO BOOK II

DIAMOND STEM/ DOLPHIN & HERONS	Readers who have one of the first 1000 books (soft cover) have the data underneath these two patterns reversed. We stopped the presses to correct this.	65
DIAMONDS, OPALESCENT	Also made in a cruet; the opalescence in this pattern is so indistinct that it is seldom sought by opalescent glass collectors.	44
DRAGONLADY	Also made in green & blue opalescent.	63
FERN, OPALESCENT	Also made in a barber bottle.	44
FLUTED SCROLLS	Also made in crystal. The spooner can either be straight-sided (smaller than the sugar base in width), or pinched in like Fig. 107.	19
GRAPE & CABLE	The punch bowl illus. is actually the large centerpiece bowl—but it is large enough to hold punch, believe me.	66
HOBNAIL & PANELLED THUMBPRINT	The tumblers to this pattern have no thumbprints at the base to distinguish them. They have 9 rows of hobs (Fig. 169 has 8), and the distinctive circle in the base.	20
HOBNAIL, 4-Footed	Also made in non-opalescent sapphire blue.	21
INVERTED FAN & FEATHER	The novelties in this pattern are *not* reproductions. They are late (circa 1920), but not new!	96
JEFFERSON DRAPE	This was made by Fenton, circa 1910 (Fig. 393)	60
JEWEL & FAN	Quite scarce in canary opalescent.	67
JEWELLED HEART	Also made in assorted novelties, including a large chop plate and smaller size plates & nappies.	22
JOLLY BEAR	Reported to me now in green & blue opales.—also in a plate!	67
KEYHOLE	Inadvertantly overlooked in the text. Fig. 432 was made at Indiana, Pa.—probably by Dugan (not Northwood as previously assumed).	74
LEAF & DIAMONDS	Note the plural last word. Scarce in green opales.	67
LUSTRE FLUTE	Also made in blue opalescent.	22
OVER-ALL HOB	Sometimes the berry set is triangular in shape.	22
PANELLED HOLLY	Also made in a salt shaker (seen only in crystal to date).	23
PINEAPPLE & FAN	The maker is A. H. Heisey—not A. J. (same mistake appears on page 11).	70
POINSETTIA	Occasionally found in white opalescent—a bowl is reported with an applied cobalt rim	45
POLKA DOT	It is now known that at least some of this was made at Northwood's Indiana, Pa. site.	45
POPSICKLE STICKS	Made in several variations—some in carnival.	70
REVERSE DRAPERY	Also made in carnival glass.	70
REVERSE SWIRL	Made also in a celery vase & night light.	45
SCHEHEREZADE	Also made in green opalescent.	71
SEAWEED, OPALESCENT	Rare in satin finish—made in 2 shape barber bottles and a miniature lamp (night lamp).	45
SIMPLE SIMON	Reported in white opalescent.	71
SIR LANCELOT	Reported with a Northwood trademark—so maker known.	71
SPANISH LACE	Also made in a miniature lamp—Northwood.	45
SPOKES & WHEELS	Several readers reported their piece marked *N*.	71
STORK & RUSHES	THE MUG WAS ALSO MADE IN CARNIVAL.	71
STRAWBERRY & DAHLIA TWIST	Quite rare in blue opalescent.	71
STRIPE, OPALESCENT	Also made in rubina—reproduced in the syrup in all colors.	46
SUNBURST-ON-SHIELD	The name was not by Hartung, but by Kamm 8, pg. 72. This is quite rare in canary opalescent.	23
SWIRLING MAZE	Note the incorrect spelling in Book 2—remember, I am basically a researcher, not a writer.	52
TOKYO	This was also made in a vase, sometimes pulled so tall that the pattern is difficult to distinguish.	24
TWIST, BLOWN	Figure 374 should be called Blown Twist to distinguish it from the pressed toy table set of the same name. The same is true of Fig. 400.	59
TWISTED RIBS	Also made in non-opalescent crystal.	72
WINDOWS (Plain)	This pattern was reproduced in a cruet (#608) and syrup—in fact, I have never seen either of these in the unswirled mold which I was convinced was old. This version of Windows—without the swirls—was also made by Beaumont (see Kamm 7, plate 59).	46
WREATHED CHERRY	I am now almost certain that this was a Dugan pattern, rather than Northwood. The carnival version of Wreathed Cherry has even been reported signed with the Dugan trademark.	24
ZIPPERS AND LOOPS	First thousand books don't have this in the text. It was made by Jefferson, circa 1903, in white, blue and green opal.	80

And there are scores of other novelties and patterns which will be listed in a later volume (sequel) which will further cover opalescent glass.

continued from page 23

FEATHER (Figure 102)
Maker: McKee primarily, with reported additional production by other firms **Y.O.P.:** from 1896 to circa 1905 **Colors made:** crystal, emerald green, amber-stained, and extremely rare in chocolate glass or blue **Items made:** too numerous to mention here **Other names:** *Doric, Indiana Swirl* **Name by:** *LEE VG*, plt. 57 **Repro's:** I am told the wine is being made **NOTE:** The syrup shown here is extremely rare.

continued from page 54

imaginable **Repro's:** none **Name by:** Orig. Mfr. name **Other name:** *Cane Shield.*

BUTTON PANEL (Figure 417)
Maker: Duncan & Sons #44 pattern **Y.O.P.:** circa 1894 with popular continued production **Colors made:** crystal & ruby-stained **Items made:** too numerous to mention—every shape imaginable **Repro's:** none **Name by:** *PET PAT*, Pg. 58.

COLUMN BLOCK (Figure 418)
Maker: Ohara's #500 pattern **Y.O.P.:** circa 1890 **Colors made:** crystal, vaseline **Items made:** Lee lists 18 different shapes (she calls it *Panel & Star*)—no toothpick or syrup **Repro's:** none **Name by:** *Kamm 3*, pg. 75.

CIRCLED SCROLL (Figure 419)
Maker: Either Northwood or Dugan at Indiana, Pa. **Y.O.P.:** circa 1903 **Colors made:** see listing Book 2 for further data **Note:** shards of this pattern were found at the Indiana, Pa. plant site, which disproves my earlier attribution to the Northwood Wheeling location. This cruet is very rare in color, and the original stopper is shaped like Fig. 408.

continued from page 55

ice—no toothpick known **Repro's:** none **Name by:** *Kamm 3*, pg. 95 **Other name:** *Divided Squares* (Metz 2) **NOTE:** The syrup in this pattern is very rare (see catalogue reprint on page 67).

HOBNAIL, FROSTED RUBINA (Figure 431)
See notes on page 27 for information regarding this pattern. This color is almost as desirable to collectors as the amberina and rubina verde.

I.O.U. (Figures 432-433)
Maker: West Virginia Glass #219 pattern **Y.O.P.:** circa 1898 **Colors made:** crystal, emerald green and vaseline **Items made:** complete table service, although most pieces are very hard to find today **Repro's:** none **Name by:** *Pet Sal*, pg. 164-C.

continued from page 56

tion after U.S. Glass merger **Y.O.P.:** circa 1890-1896 **Colors made:** crystal & ruby-stained **Items made:** complete table service—no toothpick or syrup known **Repro's:** none **Name by:** *Kamm 2*, pg. 87 **NOTE:** The *Nail* cruet is sometimes hard to recognize, since the recessed "nails" are difficult to distinguish on this piece.

OHARA DIAMOND (Figure 443)
See notes on page 34 for historical data on this pattern.

PETTICOAT (Figure 444)
See notes on page 35 for historical data on this pattern.

PINEAPPLE & FAN, HEISEY (Figure 445)
Maker: A. H. Heisey **Y.O.P.:** beginning in 1897 **Colors made:** crystal, emerald green, ruby-stained—limited custard & experimental vaseline **Items made:** every shape imaginable—some quite rare **Repro's:** none **Name by:** *Kamm 2*, pg. 93 **NOTES:** The rare syrup in this pattern is shown on page   . The Heisey name should always precede this pattern's name to avoid confusing it with another pattern which Kamm inadvertently gave the same name.

PRESSED SWIRL (Figure 446)
Maker: Uncertain **Y.O.P.:** circa 1900 **Colors made:** seen in crystal, amber & cobalt blue—possibly green was made **Items made:** not available at this time **Repro's:** none **Name by:** *Author.*

PRIZE, THE (Figure 447)
Maker: McKee for National Glass Co. **Y.O.P.:** circa 1900 **Colors made:** crystal, emerald green, ruby-stained **Items made:** every shape imaginable—including an unusual syrup **Repro's:** none **Name by:** Orig. mfr. name **NOTE:** Certain pieces of this pattern, including the cruet & syrup, lack the distinguishing thumbprints & slashes at the top of the pattern. The stopper shown in this cruet looks original, but is not (see *Kamm 6*, plate 6).

continued from page 57

U.S. RIB (Figure 456)
Maker: U.S. Glass Co. **Y.O.P.:** circa 1902 **Colors made:** crystal and emerald green **Items made:** complete table service **Repro's:** none **Name by:** *Kamm 7*, pg. 42.

X-RAY (Figure 457)
See page 46 for notes concerning this pattern's origins.

ZENITH (Figure 458)
Maker: Unknown—further research pending **Y.O.P.:** circa 1905 **Colors made:** crystal and pale blue known **Items made:** cruet & salt shakers known **Repro's:** none **NOTE:** More data on this unusual pattern will be presented in a later volume of this series.

PATTERN INDEX

This index is prepared for the first three volumes of the "Encyclopedia of Victorian Colored Pattern Glass." The pattern names are listed in alphabetical order and are followed by page numbers where pertinent information concerning it can be found. These page numbers are preceded by the appropriate volume number. For example #2-74 means that information concerning this pattern can be found in Volume II, page 74. Page numbers of illustrations are not provided as they are listed appropriately under the text to which this index refers you.

My sincere thanks to Nancy Olson for her help in preparing portions of this index.